COLONIAL
and
Revolutionary Times

A WATTS GUIDE

BY

Michael Burgan

HISTORICAL CONSULTANT

Dr. W. Guthrie Sayen
University of Connecticut

FRANKLIN WATTS
A Division of Scholastic Inc.

NEW YORK   TORONTO   LONDON   AUCKLAND   SYDNEY
MEXICO CITY   NEW DELHI   HONG KONG
DANBURY, CONNECTICUT

First American Edition 2003
Published by Franklin Watts
A Division of Scholastic Inc.
90 Old Sherman Turnpike
Danbury, CT 06816

ISBN 0-531-15453-X (Lib. Bdg.)

Library of Congress Cataloging-in-Publication Data
Burgan, Michael.
Colonial and revolutionary times : a Watts guide / Michael Burgan
    p. cm -- (Watts reference)
Summary: A guide to the major people, places, ideas, and events of colonial and
revolutionary times.
Includes bibliographical references (p.) and index.
    ISBN 0-531-15453-X
1. United States--History--Colonial period, ca. 1600-1775--Juvenile literature. 2. United
States--History--Revolution. 1775-1783--Juvenile literature [I. United States--History--
Colonial period ca. 1600-1775. 2. United States--History--Revolution, 1775-1783.]
I. Title. II. Series
    E188 .B95 2003
    973.2 03--dc21

                                                            2002027029

Printed in the United States of America.
1 2 3 4 5 6 7 8 9 10 R 12 11 10 09 08 07 06 05 04 03

Cover illustration credits:
Concord bridge battle scene (Bettmann/Corbis); Benjamin Franklin
(Corcoran Gallery of Art/Corbis); Pocahantas and son (North Wind Picture Archives).
Additional illustration credits can be found on page 144.

PRODUCED BY
Shoreline Publishing Group LLC
Santa Barbara, California

———

EDITORIAL DIRECTOR
James Buckley Jr.

———

DESIGNER
Rave &Associates

———

ART AND PHOTO RESEARCH
Dawn Friedman

———

COPY EDITOR/PROOFREADER
Carrie Gordon

Introduction

Around 1000, Norse explorers from Greenland landed in North America, becoming the first Europeans to reach that continent. The Norse did not stay at their small base in Newfoundland, Canada, but returned to Scandinavia. It took almost 500 years for Europeans to return to North America for good.

Starting in the 16th century, France, Spain, and England began establishing colonies in what is now the United States. Later, they were joined by the Netherlands and Sweden. Colonies provided wealth to European governments and businesses. They also gave adventurous settlers the chance to own large areas of valuable land. For some colonists, America offered a place where they could freely practice religions not tolerated at home.

America's colonial period was marked by wars, as Native American tribes often clashed with the Europeans invading the lands the natives had lived on for hundreds of years. Wars in Europe also spilled over to the colonies. Through these conflicts, Great Britain emerged as the major power in North America east of the Mississippi River. The descendants of English settlers controlled colonial society, and British politics shaped local governments.

Most colonial Americans were proud to be British citizens. But by 1764, as Britain began to impose new taxes, many Americans believed their rights as citizens were being denied. As Britain tried to strengthen its control, the colonists resisted. In 1775, that resistance turned to rebellion, and the American Revolution began. By 1783, the former colonists had won their independence.

Colonial and Revolutionary Times features some of the people, places, ideas, and events that shaped the birth of the United States of America. The colonial and Revolutionary eras produced both great leaders and everyday citizens, all living in a world much different from our own.

Here's a look at their lives.

Contents

John Adams

A key leader of the Revolutionary era, John Adams was a complex figure. He sometimes seemed arrogant and overly ambitious, with a blunt manner that made others dislike him. But he was also a deep political thinker, and after Americans declared their independence from Great Britain, Adams worked tirelessly for the cause. He later served the new nation as its first vice president and second president.

Adams was born in 1735 in Braintree (now Quincy), Massachusetts. After attending Harvard College, he became a lawyer, and events in the colonies drew him into politics. When Great Britain passed the Stamp Act in 1765, Adams wrote articles protesting the new tax. Like some other Americans, he believed the British could not legally tax the colonies since they lacked representation in Parliament. Adams also opposed later British efforts to raise taxes in America, although he did not support the violent protests of the taxes, which were sometimes led by his cousin, Samuel Adams.

As a lawyer, Adams believed everyone deserved a fair trial – even British soldiers. After the Boston Massacre of 1770, Adams agreed to defend the soldiers accused of killing five Americans. Adams argued that the British troops fired in self-defense, and most of the soldiers were found innocent. The two guilty men were convicted of a lesser crime than murder.

In 1774, Adams represented Massachusetts at the First Continental Congress. At the time, he did not believe the Americans colonies should be independent; he merely wanted the Americans to have the same rights as British citizens. But after the battles at Lexington and Concord in 1775, Adams realized the colonies needed their independence. At the Second Continental Congress, Adams suggested George Washington should serve as commander-in-chief of the new Continental Army.

John Adams was one of the most important political leaders of the Revolution. He later served as president of the young United States.

In 1776, Adams served on the committee that drafted a declaration of independence. When Congress debated the issue, Adams spoke for several hours, arguing passionately for independence. Afterward, Adams wrote, "I am well aware of the toil, and blood, and treasure, that it will cost us to maintain this declaration . . . yet through all the gloom, I can see the rays of ravishing light and glory."

During the American Revolution, Adams helped obtain supplies and soldiers for Washington's army. He also served as a **diplomat** in Europe, seeking support from France and the Netherlands for American independence. In 1783, Adams helped write the **Treaty** of Paris, which officially ended the American Revolution. Remaining in Europe, Adams served as the first U.S. ambassador to Great Britain. Although still abroad during the Constitutional Convention of 1787, Adams's writings on politics influenced the new U.S. government that emerged.

Adams served as the first vice president in the new government (under President George Washington) and was elected president in 1796. He was the first U.S. president to live in the White House. In 1801, after serving one term, he retired to Massachusetts.

He died on July 4, 1826, the 50th anniversary of the day Congress had approved the Declaration of Independence.

● *See also Samuel Adams, Continental Congresses, Declaration of Independence, Stamp Act, Treaty of Paris*

ABIGAIL ADAMS

In 1764, John Adams married 19-year-old Abigail Smith, and they became one of the most famous couples in U.S. history. Like her husband, Abigail strongly supported independence. She worked hard raising their five children and running the family farm while John served as a political leader and diplomat. One of their sons, John Quincy, served as the sixth president of the United States.

During John's travels, he and Abigail often wrote each other. Abigail's letters give a glimpse of life on the home front during the war. They also show her intelligent views on current affairs and the important figures of the day. Abigail opposed slavery, and some people see her as early **feminist** — a supporter of equal rights for women. *Remember the ladies*, she wrote John in 1776, *and be more generous and favorable to them than your ancestors.* Abigail died in 1818.

● ● ●

Samuel Adams

As one of the American **patriots** who most strongly objected to British rule, Samuel Adams protested against British efforts to tax the colonies and was an early supporter of independence. Thomas Jefferson called him "truly the Man of the Revolution."

A cousin of John Adams, Samuel was born in Boston, Massachusetts, in 1722. He helped run his family's brewery, although he was not skilled in business and eventually fell into debt. Adams proved better at politics, winning a seat in the Massachusetts legislature in 1765. He was already associated with the forces opposed to the Stamp Act, having helped form the Sons of Liberty, a group that often used violence to express its views on British policies. Adams soon became the leader of the **radicals** in Boston politics, speaking and writing against British efforts to control the Americans.

Samuel Adams represented Massachusetts at the First Continental Congresss in 1774 and later eagerly signed the Declaration of Independence.

In 1772, Adams declared that the British did not "have the least care or concern for the rights of Americans." The next year, he helped organize the Boston Tea Party, a protest against British policies on selling and taxing tea in the colonies. The protestors dressed like Native Americans and boarded ships in Boston Harbor. From the decks of the ships, they dumped boxes of tea into the water.

After the party, Great Britain sent additional troops to Massachusetts, and more Americans began to oppose Britain's role in colonial affairs.

In 1774, Adams wanted the colonies to unite and take action against Great Britain. He represented Massachusetts at both the First and Second Continental Congresses and eagerly signed the Declaration of Independence. Although Adams did not play a large role in government during the American Revolution, he fueled the call for independence and inspired people around New England to join the cause. After the war, he remained active in Massachusetts politics until 1797. He died in 1803.

• See also John Adams, Boston Tea Party, Sons of Liberty

Algonquians

As the first colonists settled along the east coast of North America, they met various Native American tribes now called Algonquian (al–GOHN–kwee–en). This name describes their family of related languages. One specific tribe known as the Algonquian lived in what is now southern Ontario and Quebec, Canada. The larger Algonquian grouping stretched from Maine to North Carolina and as far west as Minnesota.

Simple wooden, igloo-like huts were used by the Algonquians in their forest villages.

The Algonquian tribes had similar lifestyles as well as languages. Living in or near forests, they used trees for fuel and carved wood to make many of their tools. The Algonquian hunted deer and other forest animals, though some also fished, farmed, and collected wild nuts and berries. They built villages near rivers and lakes, but some tribes moved around searching for game or better land. Tribes within one region, such as New England or the Midwest, had more in common with each other than with tribes that lived in distant areas.

In a typical Algonquian village, families lived in **wigwams** – dome-shaped houses made with bark or animal skins stretched over a wooden frame. Long houses, longer buildings with curved roofs, were sometimes used for social and political events. Clothes were made out of animal hides or fur. For crops, farmers grew mostly corn, beans, and squash. Tobacco was used in religious ceremonies and as a medicine.

Major Algonquian tribes included the Penobscot in northern New England; the Pequot and Wampanoag in southern New England; the Powhatan in Virginia; and the Shawnee and Illinois in the Midwest. As Europeans spread across North America, they often battled the Algonquians, killing thousands. Diseases brought from Europe also killed many Native Americans. The tribes lost most of their traditional lands to the Europeans, though some Algonquian tribes are now reclaiming those lands.

Ethan Allen

Leading a group of Vermont frontiersmen known as the Green Mountain Boys, Colonel Ethan Allen won the first major Patriot victory of the Revolution. Sharing command with Benedict Arnold, Allen attacked a British fort in Ticonderoga, New York. More important than the fort itself were the cannons and other weapons Allen captured, which were later used by the Continental Army, which was what the colonial army was called.

Born in Connecticut in 1738, Allen fought briefly in the French and Indian War and then settled in what was known as the New Hampshire Grants. This land, now Vermont, was claimed by both New Hampshire and New York. Around 1769, Allen was named commander of a local **militia** – the Green Mountain Boys – to defend New Hampshire's interests from any possible New York attack.

After the American Revolution began in April 1775, Allen convinced leaders in Connecticut to support a surprise attack on Fort Ticonderoga. Allen and his men eventually met up with Arnold, who had the same mission. On May 10, the Americans took Ticonderoga. Allen marched through the fort with his sword raised, demanding to the British commander, "Come out, you old rat!" The next day, Allen won another victory at Crown Point, a smaller fort nearby.

After these successes, Allen launched an attack on Montreal, Canada. The larger British forces quickly defeated Allen's troops and took him prisoner. For part of the next three years, Allen was imprisoned in both England and New York. During this time, Vermont declared its independence from New Hampshire and New York. After his release in 1778, Allen worked to ensure that independence. Allen died in 1789, two years before Vermont became the 14th state.

● *See also Benedict Arnold*

Ethan Allen confronted the commander of Fort Ticonderoga and demanded his surrender.

Anglican Church

When English settlement began in North America, the Church of England, or the Anglican Church, was the official religion of England. The king of England was the leader of this Protestant faith, with bishops and ministers running its daily operations. The Anglican Church began in 1534, after King Henry VIII broke away from the Roman Catholic Church. The new English church kept some Catholic practices, but Anglican ministers were allowed to marry, unlike Catholic priests.

In 1619, Virginia adopted Anglicanism as the colony's official religion. In colonial America, the church was strongest there and in Maryland. In 1701, church leaders sent out **missionaries** to convert both European settlers and African Americans to the faith.

Eventually every colony had Anglican churches, but Anglicanism struggled to grow. The colonies did not have their own bishop, who could ordain, or officially appoint, new ministers. The lack of a bishop, among other reasons, led to a shortage of Anglican ministers in the colonies. The Anglicans also faced hostility from members of other Protestant faiths, who included Quakers, Congregationalists, and Presbyterians. These Protestants resisted any efforts to strengthen Anglican influence in their colonies.

As the official state religion, Anglicanism was closely tied to the British government. After 1765, many Patriots associated Anglican officials in America with Parliament's efforts to tighten control over the colonies. When the American Revolution began, some Anglican leaders became Loyalists. Others fled to Canada. After the revolution, the Anglicans remaining in the United States formed the Episcopal Church, which still exists today.

● *See also Congregational Church, Quakers, Religious Freedom*

This church in Alexandria, Virginia, was built in 1773 and attended by George Washington.

Benedict Arnold

In the first years of the American Revolution, Benedict Arnold led U.S. troops in several important battles. By the war's end, however, he was fighting for the British, and today his name is often used to refer to Americans who betray their country.

Arnold was born in Connecticut in 1741. A merchant and militia officer when the Revolution began, he volunteered to lead an attack on Fort Ticonderoga in New York. He shared command with Ethan Allen, who had recruited forces from across New England. On May 10, 1775, the Americans took Ticonderoga, capturing cannons and military supplies later used by George Washington. Arnold then moved on with a small force and captured two more British outposts. By the end of the year, he was promoted to brigadier general.

For the next several years, Arnold fought bravely in several battles. In 1776, he built a small fleet that tied up British forces on Lake Champlain, and the following year he launched a raid on a British fort in Connecticut. Later, Arnold was severely wounded at the Battle of Saratoga, a key victory for the United States.

Despite his battlefield heroics, Arnold often believed he was overlooked for promotions or treated with disrespect. These feelings led Arnold to abandon the American cause. In 1780, while commanding the fort at West Point, New York,

After his treachery was discovered, Arnold was captured. He escaped from the Americans and dashed toward British lines, where he reached safety.

Arnold plotted to give the fort to Great Britain in exchange for money. The plot failed, but Arnold escaped and became a brigadier general for the British, leading troops against Americans forces in 1781. After the war, he lived in both Canada and England. Arnold died in 1801.

● *See also Ethan Allen, Saratoga*

Articles of Confederation

Soon after declaring independence from Great Britain, the Second Continental Congress began shaping a national government. John Dickinson of Pennsylvania led a committee that drafted a document called the Articles of **Confederation**. The Articles outlined the relationship between the states and the new government. In November 1777, Congress approved the document, but it took more than three years for all the states to ratify it and officially launch the new government of the United States of America.

The Articles stated that the states had entered "a firm league of friendship with each other." Given their experience with Great Britain's Parliament, many Americans feared the power of a strong central government. Under the Articles, Congress had few powers. Most of its duties addressed declaring and waging war and conducting foreign affairs. Congress had one house, or assembly, with each state having one vote (though a state had from two to seven representatives). Nine votes were needed to approve major issues, such as entering a treaty. Other votes required a majority.

The new Congress successfully ended the war with Great Britain and prepared for American expansion into western lands. But some citizens believed the United States needed a stronger central government than the one the Articles created. Congress could not tax the states or regulate their trade. The government also had no way of enforcing the laws it passed.

The criticisms of the Articles of Confederation led to the Constitutional Convention of 1787. That meeting in Philadelphia created the national government still used today. Congress held its last session under the Articles in October 1788.

● See also Continental Congresses, U.S. Constitution

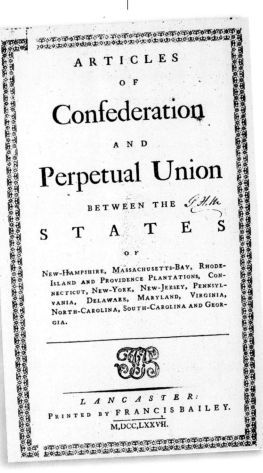

ARTICLES OF Confederation AND Perpetual Union BETWEEN THE STATES OF NEW-HAMPSHIRE, MASSACHUSETTS-BAY, RHODE-ISLAND AND PROVIDENCE PLANTATIONS, CONNECTICUT, NEW-YORK, NEW-JERSEY, PENNSYLVANIA, DELAWARE, MARYLAND, VIRGINIA, NORTH-CAROLINA, SOUTH-CAROLINA AND GEORGIA.

LANCASTER: PRINTED BY FRANCIS BAILEY. M,DCC,LXXVII.

The colonies took a step toward independence with the creation of these Articles.

Daniel Boone

Early written accounts of Daniel Boone's life made him the most famous American **frontiersman** ever. These stories were often more legend than fact, but Boone did play an important role in exploring and settling the wilderness of Kentucky.

Boone was born in 1734 outside Reading, Pennsylvania. In 1769, he and several other hunters became the first Americans to reach Kentucky, after traveling through a pass in the Appalachian Mountains called the Cumberland Gap. Boone returned to the area in 1775 with two groups of settlers.

On his second trip, Boone helped cut a path called the Wilderness Road, which many future settlers used as they moved west. Boone and the others came to Kentucky despite the Proclamation of 1763, which was a British order that forbid American colonists from settling west of the Appalachians.

In 1776, Kentucky became a county of Virginia, and Boone was named an officer in that state's militia. The Kentuckians often battled Native American tribes friendly with the British. During a battle in February 1778, Boone was captured, but he managed to escape a few months later.

Although the Battle of Yorktown in 1781 was the last major battle of the American Revolution, fighting continued along the frontier. Some British military leaders continued to encourage their Native American allies to attack the colonists. Boone served under George Rogers Clark during several major battles with these tribes.

After the war, Boone fought another series of battles, but this time in court. His land claims in Kentucky were ruled illegal, and he lost all his holdings. Boone spent most of his last years on the frontier in Missouri. He died in 1820.

Famed frontiersman Daniel Boone was one of the early pioneers of the lands west of the colonies. He remains one of the era's most famous men.

Boston Massacre

In October 1768, British troops landed in Boston to protect customs officials working for the British government. Many residents of the city hated seeing the Redcoats patrolling their streets. The tensions between the soldiers and Bostonians erupted into violence in 1770, leading to what American patriots called the Boston Massacre.

The night of March 5, a group of about 60 people taunted a British guard. One of the leaders was Crispus Attucks, a runaway African-American slave who was also perhaps part Native American. A British captain, Thomas Preston, saw the crowd growing and sent in reinforcements to help the sentry. The Bostonians responded by throwing snowballs and chunks of ice as they continued insulting the soldiers.

The mob crowded in, refusing to let the British return to their guardhouse. Some of the people hit the soldiers with clubs. One soldier fired his gun and several others quickly followed. Attucks and two other Americans died instantly; two more died later from their wounds. Patriot leaders such as Samuel Adams and Paul Revere quickly used the killings to stir up even more hatred of the British.

In October, Captain Preston and eight soldiers were tried for the March murders. John Adams helped defend them in court, and seven were found not guilty. The other two received light punishments for the lesser crime of manslaughter. By then, the troops had left Boston for a small island in the harbor.

The Patriots in Boston continued to defy British policy, however, and the soldiers eventually returned to the city. By 1775, a large British military force was in Boston, and the American Revolution was about to begin.

- See also John Adams, Massachusetts

Five Americans died in the Boston Massacre, one of the first violent conflicts of the Revolution.

Boston Tea Party

On the night of December 16, 1773, a group of Boston Patriots disguised as American Indians stormed three British ships docked in the harbor. Their mission: throw more than 300 chests of tea into the water, to protest a British tax on tea. Their successful raid became known as the Boston Tea Party.

Tea was one of the items taxed under the Townshend Act of 1767. Parliament eventually **repealed**, or removed, the tax on most items, but not tea. In response, some Americans stopped drinking their beloved beverage, while merchants smuggled tea into the colonies.

By 1773, the East India Company, the British company that controlled the tea trade, was losing money. The Tea Act of 1773 was designed to help the company by making it the only seller of tea in America; the Tea Act also kept the tax on tea sold in the colonies. The East India Company hired agents to sell the tea and collect the tax.

In the fall of 1773, ships carrying tea sailed for several American cities. Patriot protests and threats convinced most tea agents to quit their jobs, and several ships returned to Great Britain. In Boston, however, Massachusetts governor Thomas Hutchinson refused to turn back the ships.

Samuel Adams, a Patriot leader, organized protests against the tea. He and his supporters had until December 17 to take action. On that day, British officials could seize the tea from the first ship that had arrived and auction it. The day before, thousands of Bostonians met at the Old South Meeting House to discuss the situation. They tried one last time to convince the owner of one of the ships to sail it out of the harbor. He refused unless Hutchinson agreed. The governor, however, was determined to have the tea come ashore.

That evening, when Adams gave a signal, the "Indians" came to the door of the meeting house, whooping and shouting as they left for the

Protesting British taxes, a crowd of men stormed ships in Boston Harbor and dumped tea overboard.

harbor. It took about three hours for the men to empty the tea into the water. They worked silently, and took care not to harm any of the sailors on the ships. British troops knew about the raid but they did not come to the harbor. Their commander, Admiral John Montagu, did not want to risk another Boston Massacre.

After hearing about the tea party, an angry Hutchinson denounced the Patriots as criminals. John Adams had a different opinion. He called the raid "so bold, so daring, so firm…." He added that the tea party "must have…important consequences."

Boston began feeling those consequences early in 1774. Parliament closed the city's port and sent more troops to the city. These and other actions were part of the Coercive Acts (called Intolerable Acts by the colonists). Great Britain was determined to end further protests and assert its control over the colonies. Instead, the Intolerable Acts drew the colonies closer together. Americans rallied to help Boston, and political leaders called for a Continental Congress, to discuss united action against Great Britain. The Boston Tea Party played a crucial part in moving the colonies toward revolution.

● *See also Samuel Adams, Intolerable Acts, Parliament, Sons of Liberty*

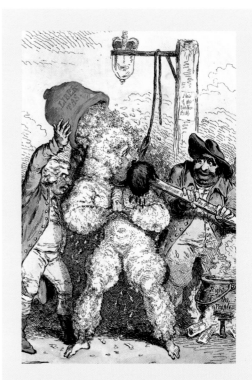

TARRING AND FEATHERING A STICKY PUNISHMENT

The Sons of Liberty sometimes targeted British officials and Loyalists with an old English punishment: tarring and feathering. The Sons poured tar over their victims, then covered them with feathers. Sometimes the feathered victims were paraded through the streets, so others could taunt them. Tarring and feathering was painful as well as embarrassing. The hot tar burned the skin, which could take weeks to heal.

● ● ●

British Army

When the American Revolution began, Great Britain had an army of about 48,000 soldiers. Not all of these forces, however, were available to serve in America. The British government hired German soldiers to help fight, and Loyalists (colonists who supported Great Britain) also joined the British cause. About 90,000 soldiers fought for Britain during the war, and they also received help from several Native American tribes.

Compared to American militias and the Continental Army, the British had better training and better supplies. They were also skilled fighting with **bayonets**. But the British army had several major disadvantages.

Parliament had to send supplies and messages across the Atlantic Ocean, which took time and money. On the battlefield, the Americans did not follow the same "rules" of war that European soldiers did. The British were surprised when Patriot troops fired at them from behind trees or rocks and attacked during the winter. Even more damaging to the British, the Americans did not have to win many battles to win the war. The Americans were prepared to retreat and force the British to chase them. Over time, U.S. leaders knew, it would be too costly for the British to continue a war so far from Europe.

● *See also Minutemen, Yorktown*

> *British troops were among the best-trained and best-equipped in the world. Their bright uniforms earned them the famous nickname Redcoats.*

Unlike U.S. forces, the British army was led by professional generals. As the war showed, however, these professionals were not always the best leaders. Great Britain had three commanders-in-chief during the war: Thomas Gage (1775), William Howe (1775-1778), and Henry Clinton (1778-1782). Another key military leader was General Charles Cornwallis. His defeat at Yorktown, Virginia, in October 1781 finally broke Great Britain's desire to fight in America.

●●●

Bunker Hill

In June 1775, American forces in Boston learned that the British planned to capture Bunker Hill in Charlestown. The hill overlooked Boston Harbor and provided an excellent spot for placing **artillery**. The Americans took action to beat the British to the hill.

The American commanders were William Prescott and Israel Putnam. Instead of putting their main forces on Bunker Hill, they set up their defense at nearby Breed's Hill. On June 17, the British launched an attack on the hill. Putnam told his troops, "Men, you are all marksmen – don't one of you fire until you see the white of their eyes." Snipers also waited for the British in local houses.

British Redcoats stormed up Bunker and Breed's Hills in the fiercest fighting to that point.

Fighting on a hot day, the British soldiers advanced slowly with heavy packs on their backs. Soon American guns began cutting them down. The British retreated and attacked again, suffering more losses.

On nearby hills and rooftops, local residents watched the battles. In the harbor, British ships fired cannonballs to try to cut down the American snipers. British general John Burgoyne described the scene: "Straight before us a large and noble town in one great blaze… and whole streets falling together in ruins to fill the air."

After launching a third attack, the British finally took the advantage. By now, the Americans were running out of bullets, and more British soldiers had arrived in Charlestown. The Americans fled Breed's Hill, suffering their worst losses during this retreat. By the end, the British also captured Bunker Hill.

Known as the Battle of Bunker Hill, the fighting that day was the bloodiest of the American Revolution. The British had more than 1,000 **casualties**, while the Americans had about 440. For the Americans, the battle boosted their confidence, even though they lost the hills. For the British, the battle showed that defeating the Americans would not be as easy as they had thought. In the future, British generals would show more caution before rushing into battle.

George Rogers Clark

A surveyor by training, George Rogers Clark explored lands west of the Allegheny Mountains. During the American Revolution, Clark used his skills as a frontiersman to lead a small U.S. force to several important victories.

Clark was born in 1752 in Albemarle County, Virginia. As a young man, Clark moved to Kentucky, where Americans were just starting to settle. When the Revolution began, Clark emerged as a militia leader, and he devised a plan to attack British forts in Illinois Country, the region that now includes Illinois and Indiana.

Clark learned that the fort at Kaskaskia was lightly defended. In 1778, he led about 175 soldiers to the fort and took it without firing a shot. With the help of French settlers in the region, Clark's men then took over forts at Cahokia and Vincennes. The British, however, soon retook Vincennes, and Clark expected the British to attack Kaskaskia in the spring of 1779. He decided to strike first, with a surprise attack on Vincennes.

The Americans and their French **allies** marched for days through flooded fields and cold rain. Despite the threat of starvation, the troops reached Vincennes in February 1779. As Clark expected, the Americans caught the British off guard. Clark tricked the British into thinking his force was much larger than it actually was. The Americans made noises and moved around, firing at the fort from all angles. Despite his losses, British commander Colonel Henry Hamilton refused to surrender – until Clark told him U.S. artillery was on the way.

The Americans had won their most significant victory in the West. For the rest of the Revolution, Clark fought against Great Britain's Native American allies and helped build American forts along the frontier. Clark's efforts helped protect American settlers in the west and gave

George Rogers Clark was one of the most important American military leaders, especially in frontier areas such as Illinois.

the United States a claim to control Illinois Country after the war. Later, his brother William explored land even farther west, as co-leader of the Lewis and Clark expedition (1804–1806). George Rogers Clark died in 1818.

Clothing

Colonial clothing came in many styles. Some of the differences depended on a person's income–the wealthy could afford to buy the latest fashions from Europe, while most Americans wore simple clothes and owned perhaps only one outfit for attending church. Religious beliefs also sometimes influenced dress – Quakers and Puritans favored simpler clothes at all times, though the wealthy often had their clothes made from better cloth. Some of the cloth used – and sometimes the clothing itself – came from overseas, though many people made their own clothing from wool sheared from their own sheep or from linen that came from **flax** grown in the colonies.

Women in the colonial era wore long skirts and dresses over a long linen nightdress called a shift. Working women wore simple skirts and a vest called a bodice. They might wear a simple cloth bonnet for a hat. The wealthy wore skirts lined with hoops to make the fabric billow out away from the body.

Men typically wore short pants called breeches, stockings to cover their legs, a shirt, and a coat or long vest called a waistcoat. On the frontier, hunters wore fringed shirts and breeches made of buckskin.

Women and girls normally wore caps like these above; gentlemen sported knee-length breeches.

Successful businessmen might show their wealth by wearing silver buttons on their coat. They were also more likely to wear fancy ruffled shirts. Most men wore simple hats with wide round brims. A familiar hat of the Revolutionary era is the tricorn, with three corners on the brim.

During the early colonial era, children were often dressed in tight clothes similar to what their parents wore. The clothes became looser during the 18th century. Both boys and girls wore dresses called frocks, though sometimes between the ages of three and seven, the boys switched to breeches or pants and a shirt.

Congregational Church

The Puritan and Pilgrim settlers of New England shared many religious beliefs. They wanted to return to a simpler form of worship, based on the ideas of a French religious thinker, John Calvin. They also believed that the members of each individual church, or congregation, should run their own affairs. No central system of bishops or other religious leaders controlled the churches. This form of Protestant religion was soon called Congregationalism, and it became the official religion in Connecticut, Massachusetts, and New Hampshire.

In early colonial times, members of a congregation who did not like how affairs were handled sometimes set off to start their own congregations. Town governments collected taxes to build and support the churches. Non-Congregationalists also paid these taxes and were not allowed to openly practice their own faiths. The churches, or meetinghouses, were the centers of social life, as well as places for worship. Church leaders were active in business and politics in their towns.

One noted Congregational minister was Jonathan Edwards. Born in Connecticut, Edwards helped lead the "Great Awakening" of the 1740s.

This movement called for deeper faith and a strict following of Calvinist teachings. The Great Awakening also affected other Protestant groups in America.

Over time, more non-Congregationalists arrived in New England. The church, however, remained strong into the early 19th century. Today, most Congregational Churches are found in New England and regions of the United States settled by New Englanders.

● *See also Anglican Church, Puritans and Pilgrims, Religious Freedom*

This Massachusetts Congregational Church has been in use since colonial times.

Connecticut

One of the smallest of the 13 original states, Connecticut played an important role during the American Revolution. The state was a key source of money, weapons, and supplies, and George Washington praised it as the "Provisions State." The name Connecticut comes from an Algonquian word meaning "beside the long tidal river."

Dutch explorers were the first Europeans in Connecticut, arriving in 1614. English settlers began coming from Massachusetts in 1633, after finding rich farmland along the Connecticut River. At first, the English had good relations with several Native American tribes, but several later wars – along with European diseases – wiped out most of these tribes.

Early Connecticut settlements were located on Long Island Sound, an arm of the Atlantic Ocean.

In Hartford, Connecticut's future capital, the Puritan settlers drafted the Fundamental Orders, describing the new settlement's government. This document has sometimes been called a kind of constitution – the first one in America. By 1665, several towns along the Connecticut River and Long Island Sound combined to form the Connecticut colony. A charter from England's King Charles II guaranteed a large degree of local political control.

For jobs, most residents farmed. A few owned slaves. The colony's location along a major river and Long Island Sound helped promote shipbuilding and trade. During the 18th century, iron mills appeared in the western part of the colony, and craftsmen built clocks and other household items.

When the American Revolution began in 1775, Connecticut immediately sent more than 3,000 troops to aid Massachusetts. Notable Connecticut military figures during the war included Benedict Arnold and Israel Putnam, a general at the Battle of Bunker Hill. Roger Sherman was a key political leader, signing both the Declaration of Independence and the Constitution.

Continental Congresses

For most of their history, the 13 American colonies acted independently. Most of the colonies' residents shared a common English culture, but they practiced different religions and had different – sometimes competing – economic interests. Still, when a crisis came, the colonies were able to act together. That political unity reached its peak during the First and Second Continental Congresses.

The first try at a meeting among colonial leaders came in 1754. Representatives from seven colonies met in Albany, New York, at the Albany Congress. The **delegates** discussed relations with Native Americans and possible joint military defense against France. In 1765, after Parliament passed the Stamp Act, representatives from nine colonies met in New York to oppose British taxes on Americans. However, these two congresses did not produce lasting results or a permanent continental association.

In early 1774, Britain passed new laws restricting freedoms in the colonies. Massachusetts, the scene of the Boston Tea Party and other protests, was particularly affected by these laws, which many colonists called the Intolerable Acts. Massachusetts called for a congress to draft a unified response to the Intolerable Acts. In September, representatives from every colony but Georgia met in Philadelphia at the First Continental Congress. These representatives included John and Samuel Adams, George Washington, and Patrick Henry.

Few members of the Congress openly called for independence from Britain. Most still saw

Independence Hall in Philadelphia was home to the First and Second Continental Congresses. These groups were the first representatives of an "American" nation.

themselves as loyal British citizens. But the representatives did want the British to respect their rights. Among other things, the Congress called for Parliament to stop taxing the colonies unfairly. The representatives also wanted Britain

Thomas Jefferson, at right, was among the important Patriots who joined the Second Continental Congress.

to remove its troops and restore local political control. The Congress approved the Continental Association, pledging not to buy goods from Great Britain until their demands were met. If necessary, the colonies would also stop selling to Great Britain.

Great Britain responded to the First Continental Congress by tightening its military grip on Massachusetts. In April 1775, British troops in the colony tried to capture military gear held by the Patriots, and fighting broke out at Lexington and Concord. In May, colonial representatives returned to Philadelphia for the Second Continental Congress. The Congress made military plans and named George Washington commander-in-chief of a new Continental Army. In July, Congress issued a statement saying, "We shall lay [our weapons] down when hostilities shall cease on the part of [Great Britain] and all danger of their being renewed shall be removed, and not before."

Even as it prepared for war, however, the Second Continental Congress discussed ways to end the conflict peacefully. It took almost another year of fighting before Congress was ready to declare American independence from Great Britain.

After July 1776, the Second Continental Congress was the government of the new United States. Its members directed the war effort, including winning support from several European nations. Congress also drafted the Articles of Confederation to create a new national government. In 1781, the Congress created under the Articles replaced the Second Continental Congress.

● *See also John Adams, Samuel Adams, Articles of Confederation, Declaration of Independence, King George III, George Washington*

Declaration of Independence

Starting in May 1775, the Second Continental Congress met in Philadelphia to discuss America's worsening crisis with Great Britain. Some members still hoped to end the conflict peacefully, but King George III and Parliament began putting more pressure on the colonies.

In August, King George III declared the colonies were in a state of rebellion and colonial leaders were traitors to the crown. During the next few months, Britain sent more soldiers and warships to break up the rebellion. In December, Parliament passed a law that cut off all trade with America. In the colonies, these steps fueled the calls for independence.

On June 7, 1776, Richard Henry Lee of Virginia introduced a resolution, or statement, for Congress to consider. "These united colonies," Lee said, "are, and of right ought to be, free and independent states." Congress delayed voting on the resolution, but it did choose a committee to begin writing a declaration of independence from Great Britain.

The committee included John Adams, Benjamin Franklin, Thomas Jefferson, Robert Livingston, and Roger Sherman. Adams, from Massachusetts, was a strong supporter of independence. He wanted Jefferson, a Virginian, to write the document. That way, Adams hoped, the British would see that independence had

Benjamin Franklin, John Adams, and Thomas Jefferson worked together with other writers to create America's most famous document.

broad support across America, not just in Massachusetts, where the rebellion had started.

Jefferson wrote for several weeks, then the rest of the committee made suggestions. On July 1, Congress debated Lee's original resolution. Some members, such as John Dickinson, still opposed independence. ". . . Our union with England," he said, "offers us so many advantages for the maintenance of internal peace." But the next day, the representatives from 12 colonies voted for independence (New York added its approval later). Congress then made many changes to Jefferson's declaration. One major change involved slavery. Jefferson had condemned King George for allowing it in America. Representatives from several states, however, demanded the sentence be removed.

On July 4, John Hancock, the president of Congress, signed the final document. He and 54 other representatives eventually signed another copy. Starting on July 8, the Declaration of Independence was read in public across the country.

Americans cheered and rang bells to celebrate their new freedom. The document's most famous lines included, "We hold these truths to be self-evident, that all men are created equal, that they are endowed by

Perhaps the most important words in the Declaration are: "…all men are created equal."

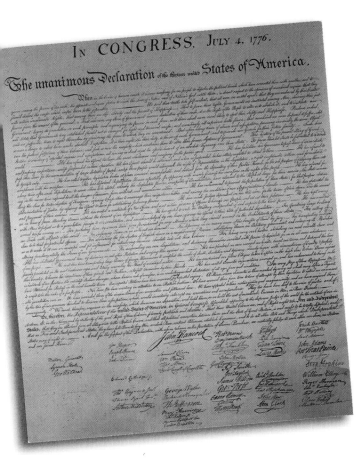

their Creator with certain unalienable rights, that among these are life, liberty, and the pursuit of happiness."

The Declaration of Independence created a new nation: the United States of America. But the Americans still had to win that independence on the battlefield.

● *See also John Adams, Continental Congresses, Benjamin Franklin, John Hancock, Thomas Jefferson, Virginia*

Delaware

The second-smallest state in America, Delaware forms a large part of the Delmarva Peninsula, which lies between Chesapeake Bay and the Atlantic Ocean. In colonial times, the area was sighted by Henry Hudson during his 1609 voyage to North America, and named for Lord De La Warr, an early governor of Virginia.

Sweden sent the first settlers to Delaware in 1638, calling the colony New Sweden. Some of these residents built the first log cabins in America, which became common on the western frontier. Two major Algonquian tribes lived in Delaware at the time: the Lenni Lenape, or Delaware, in the north, and the Nanticoke in the south.

In 1655, the Dutch took control of Delaware, then lost it to England in 1664. In 1682, William Penn of Pennsylvania acquired Delaware, despite Maryland's claims for the land. Known as the Lower Counties, Delaware remained under Pennsylvania's control until 1776, though it had its own **legislative** assembly after 1704. The colony had a diverse population, compared to other American colonies, with English, French, Dutch, Swedish, and Finnish residents, as well as African-American slaves. The commerce of Delaware was tied to wheat farming and milling, shipbuilding, and trade.

During the Revolutionary Era, Delaware produced two notable leaders. Although he represented Pennsylvania at the Continental Congress, John Dickinson lived at times in Delaware and played a role in its politics. Caesar Rodney was the colony's most vocal supporter of independence. When Congress was debating the Declaration of Independence, the Delaware delegation was split on how to vote. Rodney rode a horse through a rainstorm to Philadelphia so he could cast Delaware's deciding vote for independence.

In 1787, Delaware was the first state to approve the Constitution, earning it the nickname, "The First State."

The Old Court House in New Castle, Delaware, was built in 1732. It still flies the Swedish flag.

Family Life: Farm/Village

In 1790, the first U.S. census showed that more than 90 percent of all Americans lived on farms. For most colonial families, daily life revolved around farming. Even merchants and skilled artisans in cities and towns raised some crops or kept farm animals. A typical family produced enough food for itself and sold anything extra to pay for household items. Families also made some of their own goods, such as clothes and tools.

Every family member had chores on a farm. Fathers were clearly the "masters" of their families and the farm or business that supported them. Wives often had a large number of babies, since illness killed many infants and young children. Sons worked with their fathers to learn their skills. Daughters learned household chores from their mothers, such as making butter or weaving. At times, wives and daughters also helped in the fields. Even pets had roles to play: dogs were used in hunting, and cats kept mice

away from stored grain. Wealthier families might also own slaves, who lived with their owners, as well as paid servants to help run the household.

Older sons might leave a family farm to study or to learn a trade. The northern colonies had more towns and cities that offered job opportunities away from the farm. Daughters, if they received any education, usually learned at home from their mothers.

When not working, families pursued a variety of leisure activities. The amount of time available for fun and games depended on a family's wealth. Popular sports included boxing, wrestling, horseshoes, and early versions of baseball. Cards and backgammon were popular indoor games. Most families also attended church. Belonging to a colony's official church helped establish a family's importance in the local community.

This painting, from the 1800s, shows a rather large family farm in colonial times. The farm included a house, a barn, several buildings, and many animals.

Farming and Fishing

Colonial America was a rural society. Most people lived and worked on farms. The size of these farms and the crops raised on them varied throughout America. Most farmers grew just what they needed for their own families to survive, although the owners of plantations sold their crops in England and the West Indies. Plantations relied on slaves to work the fields. Most of these large farms grew only one crop and were located in the South, but a few northern colonies had plantations. Slaves worked on farms in every colony, but southern farmers used them more often than farmers in other regions.

In New England, farms tended to be small. The first settlers had to clear forests and dig up rocks to prepare the land. The Native American tribes introduced them to new crops, such as corn, beans, and squash. The settlers also planted crops they grew in Europe, including barley, wheat, fruits, and vegetables. Flax was another European crop grown in New England. Its fiber produced linen, which was used to make clothes. Cows and sheep grazed on land in the center of villages, called a commons, that all the farms used. Many farmers also kept chickens or other birds that produced eggs or could be served as food.

The difficulties of farming in New England led many colonists there to add fish to their diet.

New England was the main fishing region in colonial America. Shellfish, such as clams and oysters, were common along coastal waters. Fishers also sailed from many ports, including Boston, Newport, New Bedford, and New London, to the waters off Canada. Cod was the most important fish caught there. It was salted, to preserve it, and then taken to market. Much of the cod caught by New Englanders was sold to other countries. In the 18th century, many New England fishers turned to whaling. The oil found in whale blubber was used to fuel lamps across the colonies.

The Middle Colonies of New York, Pennsylvania, and New Jersey tended to have

Massachusetts and other New England states were major centers of whaling. Whales provided oil for lamps, as well as soap, food, and perfume.

larger farms than the New England colonies. By the 1750s, farmers in the region grew more wheat and other grains than the local people could use. The surplus was sold abroad. Pennsylvania was also a major producer of hay and farm animals. In some parts of New York, farmers were tenants – they rented farmland from wealthy landowners. In other colonies, tenants gave the landowners part of their crops as payment.

The major crop in Virginia, Delaware, and Maryland was tobacco. Farmers bought slaves to work on their plantations. Slaves also grew rice, the major crop of the Carolinas and Georgia. In the mid 1700s, indigo became another important crop in South Carolina. The plant was used to make deep blue dyes for clothes.

Thanks to their plantations, many southern farmers

became rich. These planters controlled the politics and economy of the southern colonies. But not all southern farmers owned plantations. Away from the coast, farms tended to be smaller, and farmers worked mostly to feed their own families, as the New Englanders did.

● *See also Clothing, Family Life, Transportation*

LIFE ON A FRONTIER FARM

During the colonial era in America, good land became harder to find along the Atlantic Coast. As the coast lands became more crowded, farmers headed for the frontier to the West. The colonies claimed land in that direction, often as far as surveyors had gone.

Frontier life was not easy. In 1711, one North Carolina farmer described his life: *I am forced to work hard with axe, hoe, and spade. I have not a stick to burn for any use but what I cut down with my own hands....help is not to be had at any rate, everyone having business enough of his own.*

● ● ●

Foreign Aid

After declaring independence from Great Britain, Congress turned to the powerful nations of Europe for help. During the American Revolution, John Adams, Ben Franklin, and John Jay were among the U.S. diplomats that went to Europe seeking money and friendship.

France was the most likely source of aid. It had lost its North American empire to Britain in 1763, and the two countries remained rivals around the world. Before the end of 1776, France secretly sent arms and supplies. Spain, France's ally, also sent supplies.

Neither France nor Spain, however, was ready to openly recognize the United States as an independent country. French and Spanish leaders first wanted to be sure the Americans could win the revolution. The U.S. victory at Saratoga, New York, in October 1777, finally convinced the French to directly support the Americans. Later, Spain declared war on Great Britain and provided some additional money to the U.S. cause, and the Netherlands signed a treaty with the Americans. But France was the crucial military ally.

A French fleet arrived in America in 1778 but did not provide much help. French assistance was more useful starting in 1780, when troops led by the Comte de Rochambeau joined George Washington's forces. The French soldiers, along with another French fleet, helped the Americans win at Yorktown, the last major battle of the war.

France and Spain did not help the Americans because they believed in the goals of the revolution. They simply wanted to weaken the British and strengthen their own empires. After the war, the United States had several conflicts with its former European allies.

● *See also Continental Congresses, Yorktown*

This engraving shows French troops landing in Rhode Island. France also provided important help with supplies and by sending naval vessels.

Foreign Generals

Looking for work or to aid the cause of liberty, a number of European military officers joined the American war for independence. At times, these foreign officers presented problems. Some could not speak English, and a few demanded that Congress give them high military ranks. But the best of these men provided crucial aid to the Continental Army during the Revolution.

The best-known foreign officer was the Marquis de Lafayette, a wealthy French nobleman. Just 20 years old when he arrived in America, Lafayette had

Poland's Thaddeus Kosciuszko was one of several European officers who helped the American army.

never been on a battlefield. Still, he was bright, brave, and dedicated to the American cause. As a general, Lafayette commanded troops during several major battles, and on a trip back to France, he encouraged his government to send troops to America.

The other major foreign figure on the American side was Baron Friedrich von Steuben. He was born in Prüssia, a part of Germany famous for its soldiers. Von Steuben was not actually a baron or a general, as he claimed to be, but during the winter of 1777-78, he trained Washington's troops at Valley Forge. Later, he fought at the Battle of Yorktown. After the war, von Steuben became a U.S. citizen.

Poland provided two noted officers to the American cause. Arriving in Philadelphia in 1776, Thaddeus Kosciuszko [koss-key-OO-skoh] served as a military engineer, helping to build forts in several states. Later in the war, he commanded cavalry troops. General Casimir Pulaski served as chief of the cavalry through the winter of 1777-78. The following year, he died from wounds he received during a cavalry charge at Savannah, Georgia.

● See also Lafayette, Valley Forge

Benjamin Franklin

A writer, scientist, politician, and diplomat, Benjamin Franklin was one of the most famous and respected figures of his era. Born in Boston in 1706, he learned the craft of printing from his brother James before moving to Philadelphia, where he started his own printing business in 1723. Franklin soon began publishing the *Pennsylvania Gazette*, one of the best newspapers in the colonies, and he also wrote *Poor Richard's Almanack*, filled with witty and wise sayings.

Franklin became a leading citizen of Philadelphia, helping to found the city's first fire department and library, a hospital, and an academy that became the University of Pennsylvania. He also worked as an inventor and scientist. His Franklin Stove produced more heat than earlier models, and his experiments with electricity made him famous in Europe.

In 1751, Franklin entered politics, winning a seat in the Pennsylvania Assembly. Three years later, when France and its Native American allies threatened the colonies, he called for the Americans to unite to handle their defense and other affairs. The plan was

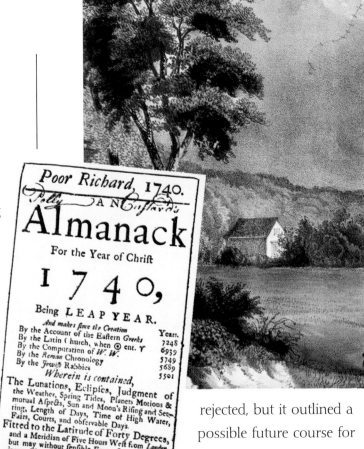

rejected, but it outlined a possible future course for American unity.

Starting in 1757, Franklin spent most of the next 18 years in London representing American interests. He helped convince Parliament to repeal the Stamp Act, and he tried to keep Great Britain and the colonies on good terms. Over time, however, Franklin opposed British efforts to tighten control of America, and although he hoped to prevent a war, he eventually supported independence.

Among the many accomplishments of Ben Franklin was the magazine-like Almanack.

Franklin was not formally trained as a scientist, but his inventive mind helped with many dicoveries.

When he returned to Philadelphia in 1775, Franklin was elected to the Second Continental Congress and later served on the committee that drew up the Declaration of Independence. After Congress approved the document he said, "We must, indeed, all hang together, or most assuredly we shall all hang separately."

In 1777, Franklin left for France, where he helped win French support for the American cause. He remained there throughout the war and for several years afterward, where he was a popular guest among the rich and famous. Along with John Adams and John Jay, Franklin **negotiated** the Treaty of Paris, which officially ended the American Revolution. Returning home in 1785, Franklin joined efforts to end slavery in Pennsylvania, then represented the state at the Constitutional Convention. He helped the delegates reach compromises and placed his esteemed reputation behind the finished document. He made the closing speech, which became the most well-known statement in favor of the Constitution.

Franklin died in 1790. In the words of one of his biographers, Thomas Fleming, "In many ways, Americans have yet to grasp the full range of his accomplishments."

● *See also Inventions, Newspapers, Philadelphia*

Free African Americans

When the American Revolution began, about 14,000 free African Americans lived in the colonies. This was less than five percent of the total African American population. Some of the earliest Africans to reach the colonies may have arrived as servants who would later be freed. They worked for up to seven years then received their freedom. These people and their descendants were the first free blacks.

Starting in the late 1600s, large numbers of Africans came to America as slaves. They could become free in several ways: earn money to buy their freedom, escape, or be freed by their masters. In a few cases, slaves in New England won their freedom in court by suing their masters. People of mixed races were automatically free if their mothers were free.

The laws affecting free blacks varied from colony to colony. In general, they could own land, and some could vote. A few became wealthy landowners, but most worked as laborers, servants, and farm hands.

As the colonies prepared for revolution, the calls for liberty and freedom convinced more whites to free slaves. Quakers led the movement to abolish slavery in Pennsylvania, and in 1780 it became the first state to gradually free its slaves. The war also gave thousands of blacks the chance to win their freedom, fighting for either the Americans or the British. After the war, the northern states slowly ended slavery, but free blacks saw their legal rights decline in the decades before the Civil War.

A FREE POET

Phillis Wheatley was one of the most famous free blacks of the Revolutionary era. Unlike most African Americans — and women — of the time, she was well educated. When she was freed by her master in 1774, Wheatley was already known as a skilled poet, often writing about religion and slavery.

•••

• *See also Jamestown, Quakers, Slavery*

Benjamin Banneker was one of the most important African Americans in early America.

Free Speech/ Free Press

In colonial America, the British government censored, or limited, some forms of speech and printed articles. People could be arrested for speaking out against government policies or printing **libel** – words that damaged someone's reputation. And colonies that had official religions limited what members of other churches could say or write.

The drive for greater freedom of speech started in the 18th century. Many Americans were influenced by English writers who believed censorship prevented people from learning the truth about their government and enjoying true liberty. Newspaper publishers such as Ben Franklin called for greater freedom of the press.

In 1735, John Peter Zenger went on trial for articles he published attacking the governor of New York. His lawyer argued that what Zenger published was true, so he was innocent. British law did not consider whether libel was true or not, but the jury accepted this argument and released Zenger. This trial is considered the first important free-speech case in America. After this decision, juries were more likely to release publishers accused of libel if what they printed were true.

Thirty years later, American newspapers felt threatened by the Stamp Act. Designed to collect taxes on anything printed on paper, the law seemed to be an attack on newspapers. Many patriot leaders supported greater press freedom, and George Mason included freedom of speech in Virginia's Declaration of Rights.

After the Constitution was written in 1787, some political leaders demanded that the new government specifically protect free speech. The First Amendment guarantees this liberty, with exceptions for such things as obscenity and speech that causes physical harm.

● *See also Religious Freedom, Stamp Act*

To keep Zenger from criticizing the government, the British burned many copies of his newspapers.

French and
Indian War

By the mid 1700s, France and England were locked in a race to acquire colonies and find riches around the world. This competition for land and resources led to a conflict that Europeans called the Seven Years' War. The part of this war fought in North America was called the French and Indian War.

In North America, France and Great Britain struggled for control of the Ohio River Valley, which included western Pennsylvania and Virginia. Both sides had allies among the region's Native Americans, and these Native Americans sometimes fought for the Europeans. Aiding the French at different times were the Ojibwa, Ottawa, Algonquian, and Delaware. British allies among the Indians included the Seneca, Cherokee, and Mohawks.

Native Americans fought with both the British and French forces during the French and Indian War. The conflict came before the Revolution.

In 1753, George Washington delivered a demand from Virginia officials for French troops to leave part of the Ohio River Valley. The French refused. Washington returned the next year to protect Virginians building a fort at what is now Pittsburgh. Before Washington arrived, the French took over the fort.

As Washington and his troops marched on, they met a small party of French and Native American soldiers. The two sides exchanged fire; it was Washington's first battle ever. The Virginians killed or wounded 11 enemy soldiers and captured 21 more. Washington then fell back and built a small fort he called Fort Necessity. The French sent a force of about 900 men to take the fort. These battles marked the unofficial start of the French and Indian War.

In 1756, after combined American and British forces lost several battles to the French, Britain officially declared war on France. During the war that followed, the two countries and their European allies eventually fought around the world. In North America, the most important battles took place on French lands in Canada. In 1758, British forces captured a French fort in Nova Scotia. The next year, the British won another major victory outside Quebec and soon after captured Montreal. When the war officially ended in 1763, Britain had won all of France's territory in North America except the city of New Orleans.

For the American colonies, the result of the French and Indian War marked a major turning point with their relations with Great Britain. Sending British troops to fight the French and Indian War had been costly. The British had also paid for supplies for the American militias that fought in the war. In the future, British

officials wanted the colonies to pay some of the cost of defending British North America. The British also tried to place new controls on the colonies. In the Proclamation of 1763, King George III declared that the colonists could not settle west of the Appalachian Mountains.

In 1764, Parliament passed the Revenue Act. This was the first of several British laws that tried to collect taxes from the colonies. Parliament believed it had the right to tax the Americans whenever it chose. Many Americans believed the British had no right to collect these taxes – especially because the Americans did not have any representative defending their interests in Parliament. Over the next decade, these conflicting views helped spark the American Revolution.

● See also Algonquians, British Army, George Washington

Games and Sports

Even the hardest-working colonists found time for games and sports. Many adults enjoyed playing cards or throwing dice, and they often gambled on the games. People also enjoyed betting on horse races and cockfights. Cockfighting was a brutal activity, as roosters tried to kill each other with steel blades attached to their legs. Other violent sports included boxing, wrestling, and cudgeling – using a long wooden stick to strike an opponent. Many wealthy and well-educated Americans did not approve of some of these activities. During the 1740s, students at Yale University were fined if caught gambling with cards or playing with cudgels.

Many games played today were popular in colonial times, though sometimes in a slightly different form. People enjoyed chess, checkers, dominoes, and backgammon. Card games included whist and cribbage. Children's games from the colonial era included hopscotch, hide-and-seek, jump rope, and marbles. Children also flew kites and raced each other while pushing large wooden hoops with a stick.

Hunting and fishing were important ways of getting food, but they were also enjoyed as recreational activities. In Virginia and Maryland, fox hunting was popular with the wealthy. Other outdoor sports included bowling and horseshoes. Dutch colonists enjoyed ice skating, and some English skated as well.

Some of the most popular sports used a bat and a ball. Cricket was the traditional bat-and-ball game. A game called town ball allowed fielders to throw the ball at runner to make an out. Town ball and cricket helped shape baseball. Although the modern game was not invented until the 1840s, the term "baseball" was used in the 1770s. At Valley Forge, George Washington's troops played an early form of baseball.

An early form of bowling like this one was introduced by Dutch settlers and became popular in many colonies.

King George III

Along with his advisors, George III shaped the policies that led the American colonies to revolt and seek independence. George was born in 1738, a member of a German royal family, the Hanovers. In 1714, Parliament had asked George's great-grandfather to rule Great Britain. George was the first Hanover king born in England. Although not very bright, he was dedicated to strengthening his country. When he took the throne in 1760, George wanted to end fighting between different political groups. He also tried to restore some of the power English kings had lost to Parliament in 1689. That year, the lawmakers had won the right to control the government.

At first George did not pay much attention to his colonies in North America. But as American protests began to increase, the king became more involved. He asserted Parliament's right to collect taxes and was ready to use the military to enforce order. For many years, Parliament and the crown had almost ignored the Americans.

George was determined to show them he was in charge.

In July 1775, a few months after the Revolutionary War started, George wrote, ". . . once these rebels have felt a sharp blow, they will submit." The king did not know the problems Great Britain would have recruiting troops and fighting a long war far from Europe. He also did not count on the Americans' strong will to win their independence. Even after the British defeat at Yorktown in 1781, George was ready to continue the war. Parliament, however, decided to end the conflict.

George ruled Great Britain until 1820. He spent most of his last years battling mental illness.

● See also Boston Tea Party, British Army, Parliament, Stamp Act, Yorktown

---

Britain's King George III sent troops to put down the Revolution, but his army was unsuccessful. At the war's end, he wanted to continue the fight, but was voted down.

Georgia

Georgia was the last British colony settled in America. Its founder, James Oglethorpe, wanted to give poor English citizens a chance to earn a decent living. British officials also saw the colony's military value, as it bordered lands controlled by France and Spain.

Georgia's early Native Americans residents included the Mississippians. They built temples and homes on huge mounds of earth; some still exist today. Later tribes included the Cherokee, Creek, Yamassee, and Yamacraw. Spanish explorers arrived in 1540. During the 17th century the British drove them out.

In 1730, Oglethorpe and some friends made plans for a new colony. They hoped to take debtors out of prison and give them land in Georgia. Instead, Parliament agreed to let poor people, but not prisoners, farm in the colony. The first settlers arrived in 1733, founding the town of Savannah. People from Germany and other European nations soon joined them.

Starting in 1740, the Georgians clashed several times with Spanish forces based in Florida. In 1742, the Spanish invaded Georgia, and Oglethorpe's forces held off the attack. The founder of Georgia then tried to attack Florida, but failed. During the next decade, the Georgians clashed several times with Spanish forces based in Florida.

Georgia founder James Oglethorpe meets Native Americans soon after arriving in the colony.

In 1752, with the colony struggling to survive, the company running Georgia turned the colony over to the British crown. Slavery was allowed for the first time, and rice plantations began to appear, as in neighboring South Carolina. By 1775, almost half of the colony's 32,000 residents were slaves.

During the Revolutionary era, Button Gwinnett was a key political leader in the colony. He signed the Declaration of Independence and briefly served as governor. During the war, British troops occupied Savannah, Georgia, until 1782.

Nathan Hale

During the American Revolution, a small-town schoolteacher emerged as one of the first heroes of the new United States. Born in 1755 in Connecticut, Nathan Hale studied at Yale before becoming a teacher. When the Revolution began, he was named an officer in the Connecticut militia and helped recruit more soldiers. Early in 1776, Hale and his troops took part in the fighting that drove the British out of Boston.

As a captain in the Continental Army, Hale next served in New York City. He led a raid in the harbor, capturing a British supply ship sitting near a much larger warship. In September, he volunteered as a spy for General George Washington, after several other officers declined the chance. A friend tried to convince Hale not to take the dangerous mission. "I wish to be useful," Hale told the friend, even though he knew "the consequences of discovery and capture in such a situation."

Posing as a schoolteacher, Hale arrived behind British lines on Long Island. He gathered the information Washington sought and was preparing to return to the American forces when he was discovered. British sailors found the papers describing Hale's mission hidden in his shoe. Some sources claim he was betrayed by a cousin who supported the British. Since he was obviously a spy, Hale did not receive a trial, and he was condemned to death. Before his execution on September 22, 1776, Hale made a short speech. He reportedly ended it with words still famous today: "I only regret that I have but one life to lose for my country."

● See also New York City, George Washington.

British troops prepare to execute captured American teacher-turned-spy Nathan Hale.

Alexander Hamilton

Although his greatest fame came during the 1780s and 1790s, Alexander Hamilton played a key role during the American Revolution. Intelligent and ambitious, he led troops in the field and served as George Washington's trusted assistant for four years.

Hamilton was born in 1755 on the Caribbean island of Nevis. He arrived in America in 1772 and soon joined the Patriot cause. In 1776, as a captain, he commanded artillery forces from New York. Hamilton and his men fought at various battles in New York and New Jersey. On March 1, 1777, General Washington named Hamilton his aide-de-camp and secretary. Hamilton wrote letters for the general and advised him on military operations.

At one point, rumors circulated that Hamilton wanted Washington removed as commander in chief. Hamilton strongly denied the charge and loyally supported the general. Hamilton left his position with Washington in 1781 but continue to serve in the military, commanding troops at Yorktown.

After the war, Hamilton practiced law in New York. He supported giving the United States a strong central government. At the Constitutional Convention of 1787 he said, "…we must establish a general and national government, completely sovereign, and annihilate the state distinctions and state operations…." Hamilton, along with James Madison and John Jay, wrote a series of articles praising the Constitution. Today these are known as the ***Federalist** Papers*.

Under President Washington, Hamilton served as the first secretary of the treasury and became the leader of one of the first U.S. political parties, the Federalists. In 1804, Hamilton died after being shot in a **duel** with Vice President Aaron Burr, a long-time political enemy.

● *See also U.S. Constitution, George Washington*

Alexander Hamilton was a successful soldier, statesman, and Secretary of the Treasury.

John Hancock

John Hancock is best known today for his bold signature on the Declaration of Independence. His name is sometimes used to refer to anyone's signature on a document. Hancock was an early supporter of the Patriot cause and a defender of the U.S. Constitution.

Born in Braintree (now Quincy), Massachusetts, in 1737, Hancock was a successful merchant who turned to smuggling after Parliament passed the Stamp Act. In 1768, his ship *Liberty* was seized by custom officials in Boston. Public protests against the seizure led the British government to send troops into the city, and Hancock began to play a larger role in local politics. He also used his vast wealth to support the Patriots. When British troops marched on Lexington and Concord in 1775, one of their goals was to arrest Hancock.

Shortly after the fighting began in Massachusetts, Hancock left for the Second Continental Congress. He was elected president of Congress. He also hoped to be named commander-in-chief of the Continental Army, but the position went to George Washington. As President of Congress, Hancock signed all the public documents the representatives issued. On July 4, 1776, only Hancock signed the original Declaration of Independence; the other representatives signed a later copy during the next few months.

In 1780, Hancock was elected the first governor of Massachusetts under its new state constitution. He won re-election several times. In 1788, he served as president of the state convention that debated the Constitution.

Hancock supposedly said that his signature was large so King George could read it without glasses.

Hancock supported the document and helped win its approval in Massachusetts. He died in 1793, while serving his ninth term as governor.

● *See also Continental Congresses, Declaration of Independence, Massachusetts*

Patrick Henry

Patrick Henry's greatest fame rests on his defiant statement of 1775. He supposedly said, "Give me liberty, or give me death." Henry was an early critic of King George III and Parliament, and he led the calls for armed resistance. He also played a key role in assuring the U.S. Constitution included a Bill of Rights.

Henry was born in 1736 in Virginia. He worked as a merchant before entering law and politics. In 1765, just days after his election to the Virginia House of Burgesses, Henry strongly attacked the Stamp Act. Throughout his political career, Henry dazzled audiences with his fiery speaking skills.

By 1774, relations between the House of Burgesses and Governor John Dunmore had worsened. Dunmore dissolved the assembly, but Henry organized the lawmakers to keep meeting on their own. In 1775, Henry led a militia that marched on Williamsburg after Dunmore had seized gunpowder from the **arsenal** there. Days later, Dunmore declared Henry an outlaw. After

spending several months in Philadelphia at the Second Continental Congress, Henry returned to Virginia to help drive Dunmore out of office.

Although Henry attended the First and Second Continental Congresses, he spent most of the American Revolution in Virginia. He served as governor from 1776 to 1779, and then again after the war. He was elected to attend the Constitutional Convention of 1787 but did not go. Henry opposed the Constitution, believing the individual states would give up too much power to the new national government. At the least, Henry wanted a guarantee of individual rights, such as free speech and legal protection in courts. He and several other prominent politicians led the fight for what became the Bill of Rights, the first 10 amendments to the Constitution.

Henry practiced law during his last years, turning

While other men fought the British with guns, Patrick Henry used his great skills as a speechmaker and debater.

down positions in President George Washington's **cabinet**. Henry died in 1799.

● *See also U.S. Constitution, Virginia*

Intolerable Acts

After the Boston Tea Party of December 1773, the British government wanted to punish the colonies, particularly Massachusetts. The next spring, Parliament passed four laws known as the Coercive [koh–ER-siv] Acts. The laws were meant to coerce, or force, the colonies into obeying British rule. The colonists soon named the laws the Intolerable Acts, meaning that the colonists just could not tolerate these new laws. Instead of forcing the Americans to give in, the laws stirred their demands for liberty.

Three of the four Intolerable Acts targeted Massachusetts. The port of Boston was closed to most ships. Local governments were virtually shut down, giving the Massachusetts governor – a British official – more power. And British soldiers and officials charged with certain crimes would go on trial in England, not Massachusetts. The fourth law, the Quartering Act, let the British quarter, or house, troops in private homes throughout America.

A fifth law was not part of the Intolerable Acts, but many Americans hated it just the same. The Quebec Act set up a new government in Canada, without local representatives or courts that used juries. The law also extended the boundaries of Canada into land claimed by some American colonies.

Many Americans rallied to support Massachusetts, which was hit so hard by the new laws. Political leaders in several colonies called for a meeting to discuss how to respond to the Intolerable Acts. At this First Continental Congress, the representatives supported a Massachusetts declaration against the Intolerable

The Intolerable Acts stirred the anger of the colonists.

Acts. Congress called the laws "unjust, cruel and oppressive." The colonies also agreed to stop importing goods from Great Britain. The Intolerable Acts and the American response brought the two sides closer to war.

- *See also Massachusetts, Stamp Act, Sugar Act*

Inventions

During the colonial era, American universities could not compare to the best in Europe. Still, the colonies produced several people with keen scientific minds and a knack for inventing.

In the 17th century, John Winthrop "the Younger," of Massachusetts and Connecticut, studied the stars with a telescope he brought from Europe. Another New England astronomer, Thomas Brattle, studied comets. Early in the 1700s, Boston's Cotton Mather learned about **inoculating** people against smallpox. Giving shots to prevent diseases was not common at the time, but Mather convinced a local doctor to try it and helped save many lives.

American settlers sometimes invented new items or improved existing ones taken from Europe. Germans in Pennsylvania developed a new kind of wagon,

Benjamin Franklin was fascinated with electricity and came up with devices to find out more about it, such as this one, which used sparks to create heat.

Franklin also designed this new type of stove. It was used in small houses for both cooking and heat.

the Conestoga, that could carry goods over rocky roads and across streams. Shipbuilders created a new kind of sailing ship, the schooner, and David Bushnell of Connecticut made the first submarine used during wartime. David Rittenhouse of Pennsylvania perfected a new pendulum for clocks. Maryland's Benjamin Banneker, a free African American, made his own clock out of wood before becoming a well-known mathematician.

The best-known American inventor and scientist of the colonial era was Benjamin Franklin. He used a kite to prove that lightning was a form of electricity, then he invented the lighting rod to protect buildings from lightning strikes. His other inventions included a more efficient stove and bifocals, glasses that helped viewers see objects both up close and far away. In 1743, Franklin helped start the first organization for colonial scientists, the American Philosophical Society.

● See also Benjamin Franklin, Ships, Transportation

Iroquois Confederacy

Some time before 1600, five Native American tribes in New York joined together to form the Haudenosaunee, or "people of the longhouse." Europeans called these united tribes the Iroquois Confederacy. The original tribal nations – Mohawk, Seneca, Cayuga, Oneida, and Onondaga – were later joined by the Tuscarora.

The effective union of the tribes impressed Benjamin Franklin. Their example influenced his call for colonial unity in 1754 at the Albany Congress.

During the 17th century, the Dutch and British made alliances with the Iroquois, creating a thriving fur trade. The Iroquois expanded their economic power by defeating neighboring tribes.

The Iroquois also had growing trade relations with the French, and after 1701 the confederacy declared itself neutral in any conflicts between France and England. That neutrality ended during the French and Indian War. In 1759, the confederacy joined the British cause.

As the American Revolution began, most of the Iroquois tribes still supported Britain, but at first the confederacy remained neutral. In 1776, a Mohawk chief named Tehyendanega – also known as Joseph Brant – stirred the Iroquois to fight for the British. Brant feared the colonists, if victorious, would take over Confederacy lands.

The Oneida and Tuscarora, however, supported the Americans. During the cold winter of 1777-1778, members of the two tribes brought blankets and corn to George Washington's troops at Valley Forge.

Starting in 1779, Washington sent troops to attack the homes of Iroquois tribes fighting against America. After the war, the Americans drove most of the Iroquois out of New York into Canada, ending the confederacy.

● See also French and Indian War, Valley Forge

An Iroquois warrior shows the typical dress and weapons of the colonial period.

Jamestown

On April 26, 1607, three ships carrying about 100 English settlers sailed into Chesapeake Bay. The settlers chose a small spot of land and called it Jamestown, in honor of England's King James I, and made it the first permanent English settlement in North America.

James I had given the Virginia Company of London the right to start a colony. Most of Jamestown's original settlers were English gentlemen hoping to trade with the Native Americans and discover gold. They were not prepared for the rigors of colonial life, and Jamestown almost did not survive.

During the first years, the settlers struggled to find food, build shelter, and fight disease. Relations with the region's Native Americans, the Powhatans, were mixed. At first, the Powhatans attacked to test the settler's military strength, but the settler's guns drove them off. Later, the Powhatans helped the English for a brief time. Relations turned violent again in 1609, leading to a five-year war.

By then, more settlers had arrived in Jamestown, including several women and craftsmen from Germany and Poland. The English never found gold in Jamestown, but they did discover that tobacco grew well in Virginia's warm climate, and that plant soon became the colony's major crop.

In 1619, Jamestown voters elected representatives, called burgesses, to serve in the first English legislative body in North America.

Political stability and the success of tobacco farming helped Jamestown grow. By 1622, the settlement had spread and included several thousand residents. That year, however, the Powhatans launched another attack. But while

One of the first tasks for Jamestown colonists after arriving on sailing ships was to construct a sturdy wooden wall around their site.

fighting broke out several more times, the English continued to arrive.

Jamestown served as the capital of the Virginia colony until 1699. Its role faded after a fire destroyed the assembly building and a new one was built in Williamsburg. But the colony's success had paved the way for future English settlement in North America.

● See also Powhatan Confederacy, John Smith, Virginia

This overhead view of Jamestown shows its protected location along Chesapeake Bay.

THE FIRST AFRICAN AMERICANS

In 1619, a Dutch ship reached Jamestown carrying about 20 Africans. The Dutch traded the Africans for food, then left. The latest records discovered from the era call these Africans slaves. What is not known is whether or not the people who owned these slaves later set them free in the New World. Other records show that free blacks lived in Virginia during the 1620s. The number of Africans in Virginia increased in the 18th century. Most were forced from their homelands to work as slaves on tobacco plantations.

● ● ●

John Jay

John Jay was one of the first great U.S. diplomats. Along with Benjamin Franklin and John Adams, Jay helped negotiate the Treaty of Paris, which ended the American Revolution. More than a decade a later, he signed a treaty with Great Britain that bears his name.

Born in 1745, Jay came from a wealthy New York family. He was practicing law when he was chosen in 1774 to attend the First Continental Congress. At that time, Jay hoped the Americans could peacefully settle their conflict with Great Britain. By 1776, however, Jay backed independence.

In 1777, Jay helped write the first state constitution for New York. He then served briefly as the president of the Second Continental Congress before starting his diplomatic career. His mission: convince Spanish officials to formally support the United States and recognize its independence. Jay spent more than two years in Spain. While he was there, the Spanish government gave the United States some secret aid, but Jay never won the official recognition the Americans sought.

In the summer of 1782, Jay arrived in Paris to begin peace talks with Great Britain. He distrusted the French, and he did not want to follow their advice on how to negotiate the treaty. In November 1782 he wrote, ". . . it is not their interest that we should become a great and formidable people, and therefore they will not help us to become so." Congress had instructed Jay and the other American officials sent to Paris to work with the French, but Jay ignored this order. He pushed for Britain to recognize U.S. independence. Adams and Franklin supported this position.

John Jay contributed his talents and intelligence to the new nation in many ways. He was a writer, diplomat, representative, and judge.

In the final Treaty of Paris, the British did recognize U.S. independence.

Returning to the United States, Jay served as secretary of foreign affairs. He did not attend the Constitutional Convention of 1787, but he did support the new government it created. In 1789, President George Washington named Jay the first chief justice of the Supreme Court. Five years later, he went to Great Britain to try to end a growing crisis.

In 1793, the British began seizing U.S. ships trading in the West Indies. U.S.–British relations were also strained because British troops were still at several forts in the Northwest, the region west of the 13 states and east of the Mississippi River. In the Treaty of Paris, the British had agreed to remove these soldiers. Jay's job was to stop these issues from leading to another war. In Jay's Treaty, signed in 1794, the British said they would leave the Northwest. The two countries also agreed to better trade relations.

In 1795, Jay left national politics and served as governor of New York for several years. Throughout his career, he was known for his honesty and dedication to his country. Jay died in 1829.

- See also Foreign Aid, Treaty of Paris

See also Foreign Aid, Treaty of Paris

FEDERALIST AUTHOR

In 1787, John Jay joined Alexander Hamilton and James Madison in writing newspaper articles supporting the Constitution. These articles are now called the *Federalist Papers* (below). Jay wrote a strong national government would limit the risks of foreign attacks. "…one government, watching the general and common interests and combining and directing the powers and resources of the whole, would … conduce far more to the safety of the people."

• • •

THE
FEDERALIST:
ADDRESSED TO THE
PEOPLE OF THE STATE OF
NEW-YORK.

NUMBER I.
Introduction.

AFTER an unequivocal experience of the inefficacy of the subsisting federal government, you are called upon to deliberate on a new constitution for the United States of America. The subject speaks its own importance; comprehending in its consequences, nothing less than the existence of the UNION, the safety and welfare of the parts of which it is composed, the fate of an empire, in many respects, the most interesting in the world. It has been frequently remarked, that it seems to have been reserved to the people of this country, by their conduct and example, to decide the important question, whether societies of men are really capable or not, of establishing good government from reflection and choice, or whether they are forever destined to depend, for their political constitutions, on accident and force. If there be any truth in the remark, the crisis, at which we are arrived, may with propriety be regarded as the æra in which that

Thomas Jefferson

"As long as we may think as we will," Thomas Jefferson wrote, "and speak as we think, the condition of man will proceed in improvement." Jefferson believed people had a natural right to think and speak as they chose and to govern themselves. Although he held several important political positions – including U.S. President – Jefferson was most comfortable with books, exploring science, history, religion, and many other intellectual interests. He was one of the greatest thinkers of his era.

Jefferson was born in Virginia in 1743. A curious student, he delayed starting a law practice so he could continue his studies. Jefferson lacked the speaking skills to be a great lawyer, and he did not like conflict – whether on the battlefield or in a room filled with debating politicians. But he was a forceful writer and believed Americans should assert their natural right of liberty.

In 1774, as a member of the Virginia House of Burgesses, Jefferson wrote *A Summary View of the Rights of British America*. This document, his first published work, convinced the Second Continental Congress to place Jefferson on the committee that drafted the Declaration of Independence. John Adams, one of four other committee members, suggested Jefferson should actually write the document.

For several weeks, Jefferson wrote in a rented room. He usually worked standing up and sometimes wrote late into the night. Later Jefferson said he wanted the declaration to be "an expression of the American mind." The other members of his committee made some changes to the Declaration of Independence, as did Congress. But on the whole, Jefferson was the draftsman of one of the world's greatest political statements ever.

After writing the Declaration and helping lead America into nationhood, Jefferson became the third President of the United States.

For most of the Revolution, Jefferson stayed in Virginia. In 1779, he wrote the state's law guaranteeing religious freedom. Jefferson considered this one of his three greatest accomplishments. (The other two were drafting the Declaration of Independence and founding the University of Virginia.)

Jefferson served as governor of Virginia before returning to Congress in 1783. Jefferson was in France, serving as a diplomat, when the Constitutional Convention met in 1787. Jefferson strongly supported adding a bill of rights to the Constitution to protect individual freedoms.

In 1790, Jefferson joined President George Washington's cabinet as secretary of state. Under President John Adams, Jefferson was Vice President. During the 1790s, Jefferson emerged as the leader of a new political party, the Republicans. In general, they opposed giving the national government strong powers. Jefferson was elected the third U.S. president in 1800 and served two terms.

Jefferson spent his last years at his home, Monticello. He wrote letters to many friends, including Adams. The two Revolutionary leaders were political enemies for a time, but they repaired their relationship.

Jefferson died on July 4, 1826–the 50th anniversary of the approval of the Declaration of Independence. John Adams died the exact same day.

- *See also Declaration of Independence, U.S. Constitution, Virginia*

JEFFERSON AND SLAVERY

Thomas Jefferson had conflicting ideas about slavery and African Americans. In the Declaration, Jefferson wrote "All men are created equal," but he owned slaves and believed blacks were "inferior to the whites in…both body and mind." Jefferson wanted slaves freed at some point. Then he suggested they be educated and sent back to Africa.

• • •

This statue of Jefferson stands in the memorial to him in Washington, D.C.

John Paul Jones

Although uneducated and eager for personal glory, John Paul Jones was also a skilled sea captain. His daring raids during the American Revolution made him the first U.S. naval hero.

Born in Scotland in 1742, Jones was first known as just John Paul. He started sailing at 12 and within 10 years was captain of a merchant ship, sailing often to the West Indies. After killing a rebellious crew member in 1773, he fled to America to avoid criminal charges, and added "Jones" to his name. Jones was unemployed when the Revolutionary War started, but he won a position as lieutenant in the Continental Navy.

In 1776, Jones received his first command, of the *Providence.* With a small fleet, Jones captured more than a dozen British ships and was quickly promoted to captain. In 1778, sailing the *Ranger* out of France, Jones raided the English town of Whitehaven and captured several British vessels. The next year, the French gave him a larger ship, which Jones named *Bonhomme Richard.*

On September 23, 1779, Jones encountered a fleet of British merchant ships protected by two warships. In a long battle, Jones defeated the *Serapis.* At one point, the British ship and the *Bonhomme Richard* were side by side. The British captain asked Jones if he wanted to surrender. He supposedly replied, "I have not yet begun to fight." Jones captured the enemy, though his own ship sank. The victory made him a hero, but the British considered him a pirate.

Jones returned to America in 1781, but eventually returned to Europe. In 1787 during his last visit to the United States, Jones received a gold medal from Congress. He was the only officer in the Continental Navy to earn that honor.

Jones later served in the Russian navy and lived in France. He died in Paris in 1792. In 1905, the remains of his body were taken to the United States and are now buried at the U.S. Naval Academy in Annapolis, Maryland.

John Paul Jones was America's first naval hero and the most famous fighting sailor of the Revolution. His victories over the British made him a national hero.

Henry Knox

Henry Knox commanded the artillery troops of the Continental Army throughout the American Revolution. Born in Massachusetts in 1750, Knox operated a bookstore in Boston when the war began. As a teenager, he joined the local militia and educated himself about artillery weapons. In 1770, he saw the Boston Massacre, and by one historian's account, he tried to prevent a British soldier from firing into the angry crowd. Five years later, Knox volunteered to help General Artemas Ward at the Battle of Bunker Hill. Before the end of the year, George Washington picked Knox to lead the artillery. He became one of Washington's most trusted advisors and was known for his good relations with his men.

Knox's first mission was to get the artillery pieces captured at Fort Ticonderoga, New York, to the American troops in Boston. Knox and his men used sleds and teams of oxen to transport almost 60 large guns over snow-covered roads, mountains, and frozen rivers. The heaviest of the weapons weighed one ton each. The soldiers also moved more than a ton of lead to be used as ammunition. Knox made the 300-mile trip in about six weeks. In March 1776, Washington stationed the largest guns on Dorchester Heights, overlooking Boston. British general William Howe decided to leave the city rather than attack the guns, which threatened British ships.

As the war moved into New York and New Jersey, Knox and his troops performed well at several battles, including the victory at Trenton. Knox was promoted to brigadier general at the end of 1776. He was with Washington at Valley Forge during the winter of 1777–1778, and he commanded the artillery at Yorktown in 1781. The next year, Knox took control of the fort at West Point,

> Knox was a good friend of George Washington and one of his top aides. Knox also was the leader of America's artillery forces in the Revolution.

New York. He later served almost ten years as secretary of war. Knox died in 1806.

- See also Ethan Allen, George Washington, Valley Forge, Yorktown

Marquis de Lafayette

General George Washington received help from many Europeans during the American Revolution, but he grew close to just one. Washington wrote, "I do most devoutly wish that we had not a single foreigner among us, except the Marquis de Lafayette."

Marie-Joseph, the Marquis de Lafayette, was born in France in 1757. From a wealthy family, he entered the army when he was a teenager. In 1776, he decided to fight for the Americans. Lafayette wanted to battle France's traditional enemy, Great Britain, and win glory for himself. At first the young officer did not particularly support American political ideals, but over time he cherished them.

Lafayette reached America in 1777 and volunteered to serve under Washington. Although just 20 years old, Lafayette quickly won the respect of the troops. He fought bravely and was wounded at the Battle of Brandywine,

and he never complained about the harsh conditions at Valley Forge. With Washington's support, Congress gave Lafayette his own command. He hoped to lead an invasion of Canada in 1778, but he lacked the troops and supplies he needed for the mission. The next year, he went to France and convinced French leaders to give the Americans more aid.

Lafayette returned to the United States in 1780. Washington sent him to command troops in Virginia, and his forces fought several major battles. After fighting in the Battle of Yorktown, Lafayette returned to France.

During the war, Lafayette spent about $200,000 of his own money to supply American troops. In 1803, Congress gave him more than 11,000 acres of land to thank him for his service. Years later, Lafayette toured the United States and received a hero's welcome.

● See also Foreign Generals, Foreign Aid, Valley Forge, Yorktown

The French officer the Marquis de Lafayette combined great military skills with a love of American ideals to become a key member of George Washington's staff.

Lexington and Concord

Early in the morning of April 19, 1775, the growing conflict between the British government and patriots in Massachusetts erupted in bloodshed at the towns of Lexington and Concord. Soon after, the other colonies united to help Massachusetts fight the British. A little over a year later, the colonies formally announced their independence and created a new nation – the United States of America.

On that April morning, about 700 British troops, sometimes called Redcoats, marched from Boston to Concord, looking to capture military supplies the colonists had stored there. The night before, several riders, including Paul Revere, had warned the towns along the route to Concord about the British plan. On the 19th, when the British reached Lexington, they found about 70 minutemen waiting at the town green.

These patriot soldiers were led by Captain John Parker. He supposedly told his troops, "Don't fire unless fired upon, but if they mean to have a war let it begin here." A shot rang out; it's not clear which side fired it. Then the two forces exchanged fire, and eight patriots were killed. The Redcoats continued on to Concord, where more minutemen gathered. In another exchange, the British killed two Americans while losing three of their own.

Then the Redcoats began the long march back to Boston. Along the road, minutemen hid behind buildings, trees, and rocks, attacking the British. When the British troops finally reached Boston, they had suffered about 270 casualties, while the Americans had about 90.

Despite some efforts between the two sides to prevent more fighting, the Battle of Lexington and Concord marked the start of the American Revolution.

● See also British Army, Minutemen, Paul Revere

Where it all began: British and American forces first fought at a bridge in Concord, Massachusetts.

Loyalists

As American Patriots resisted British colonial policies, another group of Americans supported Great Britain and opposed independence. These people were called Tories or Loyalists. Notable Loyalists included Governor Thomas Hutchinson of Massachusetts and Pennsylvania merchant Joseph Galloway.

The Loyalists came from every colony and many different backgrounds. Some worked for the British government and did not want to lose their jobs. Others opposed breaking ties with Great Britain, even if they did not support all of Parliament's actions. And some feared change and the kind of government the Patriots might establish in an independent America. By some estimates, as many as one-third of the colonists considered themselves Loyalists.

After the American Revolution began, the new state governments often seized Loyalists' property. A few Loyalists were beaten by Patriot mobs – a practice that started before the Revolution. Some Loyalists fled America, but tens of thousands stayed to help the British fight. Other Loyalists served as spies or provided supplies. Still, the British never had as much Loyalist aid as it would have liked.

When the war ended, Congress told Great Britain it would restore the Loyalists' property and legal rights. In most cases, the Loyalists regained their rights, but not their property. Some were also threatened or killed by angry Patriots.

As many as 80,000 Loyalists left America during and after war. Most went to Great Britain and Canada. About 35,000 settled in Nova Scotia, including several thousand freed African American slaves who supported Great Britain.

● *See also King George III*

As the Revolution heated up, colonists who remained loyal to Britain were often treated rudely. Below, the "loyalist" in red is being carried out of town on a rail.

James Madison

James Madison won national prominence at the Constitutional Convention held in 1787 after the Revolution. Sometimes called the "Father of the Constitution," Madison strongly supported that document and wrote the Bill of Rights.

Madison was born in Virginia in 1751. Unlike many wealthy Virginians, he preferred books to hunting, riding, and other social activities. After graduating from the College of New Jersey (now Princeton University) in 1771, Madison returned home and entered politics. In 1776, he attended the convention that created Virginia's first state constitution, and he called for broad support of freedom of religion. Madison was elected to the Continental Congress in 1779. He began to see the need for a stronger central government.

In 1786, Madison attended the Annapolis Convention, called to discuss problems with the government created by the Articles of Confederation. Madison and Alexander Hamilton led the call for another convention to revise the Articles. At the Constitutional Convention of 1787, Madison backed the Virginia Plan, which he had helped create. This called for each state to send a number of representatives to Congress based on their population. Madison also wanted two houses in Congress and three separate branches of government: legislative, executive, and judicial. Madison served on the committee that wrote the final document.

Once the Constitution was written, Madison joined John Jay and Alexander Hamilton in writing newspaper articles supporting the new government. These articles are now called the *Federalist Papers*. Madison also supported a bill of rights to prevent the government from taking away individual rights. "Wherever there is an interest and power to do wrong," Madison wrote, "wrong will generally be done."

In the new government, Madison served in Congress for 10 years and as secretary of state under President Thomas Jefferson. In 1809, Madison was elected the fourth U.S. president and served two terms. He died in 1836.

- See also Alexander Hamilton, John Jay, U.S. Constitution, Virginia

After helping to develop Virginia's constitution, Madison helped draft the U.S. Constitution. He became president in 1809.

Francis Marion

General Francis Marion was known as the "Swamp Fox" for his skill at moving through the swampy waters of rural South Carolina. He was born in that colony around 1732. His first military experience came in 1761, fighting Native Americans on the frontier. By 1775, Marion was a successful plantation owner, but he returned to the battlefield to help South Carolina's Patriots defend Charleston from British attack.

The first few years of the American Revolution were fought mostly in the north. As the war moved south, Marion fought at several major battles. In 1779, he led troops at Savannah, Georgia. The next year, he was forced to leave Charleston as the British took control of the city. Marion then became one of several South Carolina officers who used guerrilla warfare to harass the British. Striking with small forces, Marion and his troops attacked swiftly then retreated into the woods. One British officer complained that Marion "would not fight like a gentleman." Several times, the Swamp Fox launched attacks even though he was outnumbered, counting on his ability to surprise the enemy. During one raid, he freed about 150 U.S. troops being held prisoner.

In 1781, Marion worked with forces led by Henry "Light-Horse Harry" Lee to capture Fort Watson and Fort Motte. The victories were part of a large **campaign** to drive the British out of South Carolina. Although his troops did not

Francis Marion (right) meets with his men in a swamp. Marion's knowledge of these lands made him a hard man to defeat.

always win, Marion was respected for his bravery and ability to lead soldiers in battle. After the Revolution, Marion held several positions in South Carolina's government. He died in 1795.

● *See also South Carolina*

Maryland

In 1632, the Calvert Family of England received royal permission to start a colony along the Chesapeake Bay, just north of Virginia. King Charles I named the colony Maryland, in honor of his wife. The English settlers of Maryland found many different Native American tribes along the Chesapeake. These included the Nanticoke, Potapaco, and Choptank. The settlers had fairly good relations with Native Americans.

The Calverts were Roman Catholic, and their faith was under attack in England. The Calverts wanted all Marylanders to have religious freedom. In 1649, the colonial assembly passed the first law in America guaranteeing this freedom for all Christians. Over time, however, Protestants took control of Maryland's government, and Anglicanism became the colony's official religion. In fact, they discriminated against Catholics.

By the early 1700s, Maryland's economy was based largely on tobacco farming. Large numbers of African-American slaves were brought to work plantations in the southern part of the colony. Slavery was less common in the north and west, where people farmed much smaller plots. During the mid-18th century, Baltimore became an important port and center for shipbuilding. Trade with other colonies and the West Indies fueled growth there.

During the American Revolution, Maryland's troops fought bravely and were called the "Old Line." Today one of Maryland's nicknames is "the Old Line State." The state's political leaders included Charles Carroll and Samuel Chase, two of the state's four signers of the Declaration of Independence. Chase later served on the Supreme Court. In 1781, John Hanson of Maryland was chosen the first president of the new Congress created by the Articles of Confederation. At the end of the war, Annapolis briefly served as the U.S. capital.

● *See also Other British Colonies, Religious Freedom*

An early trading post on Kent Island was located on Chesapeake Bay. Small settlements like this were the way Maryland and other colonies began.

Massachusetts

The first English settlers of Massachusetts came seeking religious freedom. More than a century later, Massachusetts citizens led the way to political freedom for all Americans in the English colonies.

In November 1620, Puritan settlers now known as the Pilgrims reached Cape Cod, and then started a colony in Plymouth. This was the first permanent English colony in New England. With help from the Wampanoag Indians, the settlers survived their first difficult years in America. Later, however, the English clashed with the Wampanoag and other local tribes, taking their lands.

In 1630, a group of Puritans led by John Winthrop arrived in Boston from England and founded the much larger Massachusetts Bay Colony. The Puritan, or Congregational, faith was the colony's official religion. To train future ministers, the Puritans started Harvard, America's first college, in 1636.

From Boston, Puritan settlers spread along the coast and into the western part of Massachusetts. Boston, however, remained the center of politics and commerce. The two colonies of Plymouth and Massachusetts Bay were later merged into one, with the governor appointed by the English king. Local political control, however, remained strong in cities and towns.

In most towns, people supported themselves by farming and making their own goods. Timber was cut and sold outside the colony, and Massachusetts was the center of America's fishing industry. By the 1700s, many Boston merchants and ship owners were making sizable fortunes. Some of the businessmen transported

and sold African slaves, though the number of slaves who lived in the colony was small.

When Great Britain passed the Stamp Act in 1765, Massachusetts residents protested strongly. Samuel Adams led the efforts to resist this law and other new British taxes. In 1768, he wrote a letter to all the other colonies, calling for them to unite against unfair taxes.

As Boston became a center for Patriot anger, Great Britain responded by sending troops to the city. The British also continued to tighten its control over Massachusetts and the other colonies. After the Intolerable Acts of 1774, Massachusetts once again called for a united colonial response against the British. This led to the First Continental Congress.

In April 1775, British troops clashed with Massachusetts militiamen at the towns of Lexington and Concord. The American Revolution had begun, and for almost a year, fighting took place in and around Boston. By the next March, however, the British left. The state continued to play an important role in the Revolution, providing many political leaders. The most influential was John Adams, a dedicated Patriot and keen political thinker.

• See also Samuel Adams, Boston Massacre, Boston Tea Party, Intolerable Acts, Lexington and Concord, Puritans and Pilgrims, John Winthrop

Native Americans greet settlers on the Charles River, near what is today Boston, Massachusetts.

A colonial-era windmill in Massachusetts.

BIRTHPLACE OF THE REVOLUTION

In the years before the American Revolution, several events in Boston weakened the ties between Great Britain and its colonies. In 1770, the Boston Massacre left five Americans dead, and showed the anger Bostonians felt over seeing British Redcoats patrolling their streets. Three years later, the Boston Tea Party was the largest Patriot protest yet against taxes. Britain responded by once again sending troops into Boston and limiting local control of the government. Those acts stirred Americans in every colony to help Boston resist policies that George Washington called "repugnant to every principle of natural justice."

•••

Medicine/Disease

Colonial America had few doctors who studied in schools. Most healers started as apprentices, learning from more experienced doctors. (Some colonists learned about healing plants from Native Americans.) Medicine in general was very primitive during the 17th and 18th centuries. For many illnesses, doctors bled their patients or forced them to vomit. Doctors thought these methods removed whatever was making a patient ill. Some herbs were effectively used as medicine. Doctors set broken bones or performed simple surgery, though patients usually suffered greatly or died from infections. **Midwives** usually helped pregnant women deliver babies.

The Europeans who settled in North American brought several diseases with them. One of these was smallpox. Since the disease was new to the region, Native Americans did not have any resistance, or ability to fight off the disease. Smallpox killed tens of thousands of Native Americans. The disease could also be deadly to the settlers. In 1721, Zabdiel Boylston of Boston was the first doctor to inoculate patients against smallpox. He took a small amount of pus from the open sore of a person already infected and injected this into healthy patients. African American slaves sometimes performed similar inoculations. Other common diseases included tuberculosis, which affects the lungs, malaria, and yellow fever. These last two come from the bite of certain mosquitoes. These diseases were once common in warm climates.

America's first medical school opened in Philadelphia in 1765. That city was also the home of one of the most famous American doctors, Benjamin Rush. He helped improve the care of mental patients and fought a yellow fever epidemic that struck Philadephia in 1793.

Even in colonial days, taking a patient's pulse was part of any medical exam. Here a doctor uses a pocket watch to help count the heartbeats.

Metacom

Metacom was the **sachem**, or leader, of the Wampanoag tribe of eastern Massachusetts. The English settlers called him "King Philip." Metacom (sometimes spelled Metacomet) was the son of Massasoit, the sachem who helped established peaceful relations between his people and the Pilgrims of Plymouth. By the late 1660s, however, Metacom realized the English threatened his people's land and existence. He criticized colonial laws that prevented Native Americans from living as they had before the settlers came. Several times, the English brought Metacom to Plymouth and accused him of treason, but each time he defended himself and was released.

Starting in 1671, Metacom began asking other tribes for their support in case of a war against the English. Meanwhile, relations with colonists worsened. In 1675, three Wampanoag were executed for murdering another Native American who had become a Christian. In June, an isolated Wampanoag attack on a village quickly turned into a war against colonists in Massachusetts, Rhode Island, Maine, and Connecticut. Metacom's allies included the Narragansett and the Nipmuc. The English called the conflict King Philip's War.

Through the rest of the year, Indian forces raided dozens of English villages, but by 1676, the Wampanoag began to run short on food. The colonists, aided by several Native American

Also known as "King Philip," Metacom was one of the leaders of the Native American resistance.

allies, including the Mohegan and the Mohawk, successfully counterattacked. In August, Metacom was killed at a battle near his home. His wife and 9-year-old son had already been captured and sold as slaves.

More than 3,000 Indians and 600 settlers died during King Philips' War. The defeated tribes were nearly wiped out, and the English never faced another major attack in New England.

Minutemen

In September 1774, the political leaders of Worcester County, Massachusetts, disbanded their local militia, wanting to eliminate any Loyalist influence among the troops. The county formed a new militia and gave one-third of the men a new responsibility. They had to be armed and ready to fight with just one minute's notice. Soon, militia across Massachusetts added "Minutemen" to their ranks.

Recruiting the Minutemen was not always easy. The town of Concord needed several months to convince local men to join the new service, since the pay was low. Eventually, the town reached its goal of about 100 soldiers, most of them under 25 years old. The Minutemen elected their own officers. Some of the officers had military experience from the French and Indian War. Most of the enlisted men were young farmers or tradesmen. In some cases, they did not own their own guns and had to borrow them.

The Minutemen saw their first battle on April 19, 1775, at the Battle of Lexington and Concord. British troops marched out of Boston, looking to capture military supplies stored in Concord.

Given advance warning, the local Minutemen and militia were waiting for the British as they reached Lexington. The two sides exchanged shots there and in Concord. One Minuteman said their orders were "not to fire till [the British] fired first, then to fire as fast as we could." The worst casualties came during the British retreat to Boston, as Minutemen and militia fired at them while hiding behind walls and inside buildings.

After this first battle of American Revolution, several other colonies recruited their own Minutemen. In Massachusetts, they formed part of the new Continental Army that eventually forced the British out of Boston. Although the Minutemen did not serve long, they became a symbol of the colonists' readiness to fight for independence.

● *See also Lexington and Concord; Paul Revere*

Although they were often new to the military, America's Minutemen proved to be victorious against the mighty British Army.

Mohawk

One of the tribes in the Iroquois Confederacy, the Mohawk lived in upstate New York. For centuries before the Europeans reached North America, the Mohawk hunted, fished, and gathered wild nuts and berries. They also farmed, raising corn, beans, and squash. Clans lived in houses up to 200 feet long and 25 feet wide, with round roofs covered with bark.

The Dutch were the first Europeans to reach upstate New York, and they traded with the Mohawk and the other Iroquois tribes. By the end of the 17th century, the British and French dominated the region. The Mohawk were particularly close to the British. In 1710, their sachem (chief) Hendrick traveled to London, and he fought for the British in the French and Indian War. Hendrick also advised the American colonists to copy the Iroquois and unite in a confederacy.

At the start of the American Revolution, the Iroquois officially said they would not help either the British or the Americans. The Mohawk, however, clearly favored the British. Their chief, Theyendanegea (also called Joseph Brant), was related by marriage to a British official and had joined the Church of England. Brant wanted all the Iroquois to fight the Americans. In 1777, Brant led a force of Iroquois warriors in a joint attack with the British against the Americans. On the American side were about 60 Oneida–also members of the Iroquois confederacy. The American Revolution split apart the Confederacy. After the war, Brant and most of the remaining Mohawk settled in Canada.

● See also Iroquois Confederacy, New York

A Mohawk village in central New York state contains both huts and buildings.

Music, Dancing, and Theater

For much of the 17th century, most people living in America did not have the time or money to spend on the performing arts. Religion also played a part in limiting public entertainment. In New England and Pennsylvania, plays and most public dancing were outlawed because they were considered immoral. Even after the laws changed, some religious leaders spoke against these art forms. But members of all faiths welcomed singing in church.

Music, dance, and theatre became more popular in the 18th century. Singing was part of daily life at celebrations and helped workers pass the time at their jobs. African slaves and European settlers brought musical traditions from their homelands to America. Educated people were expected to play at least one instrument, such as a keyboard instrument, the violin, or the flute. After the 1730s, wealthy citizens in several cities started musical societies that sponsored concerts. Most musical pieces and songs were by European composers, though Francis Hopkinson and William Billings were two noted American songwriters.

The styles of dancing varied in the colonies. In Virginia and other southern colonies, social life centered around balls. These formal parties could last for several days, and the dances and music were often borrowed from France. In other regions, and especially among working people, country dances from Great Britain were popular.

For theater, Americans usually saw plays by English playwrights, such as William Shakespeare. The first theater companies featured actors from

Fancy-dress balls in colonial times often featured dances to European classical music.

England who traveled to different cities. The first native theatre company formed in Philadelphia in 1749, and American playwriting did not really start until just before the American Revolution. The first major playwrights included Thomas Godfrey and Mercy Otis Warren.

New Hampshire

English traders and fishers reached New Hampshire in the early 1600s, but settlers did not arrive until 1623. The first few towns appeared along New Hampshire's southern seacoast, just north of Massachusetts. The Native Americans of the region belonged to various Algonquian tribes. During most of the 17th century, the Penacook were the largest of these tribes.

New Hampshire's early political life was marked by turmoil. For a time, New Hampshire was part of Massachusetts. Many of the first settlers had come from there. At the end of the 17th century, control of the colony fell to relatives of Captain John Mason, who had been awarded most of New Hampshire in 1629. Later, the colony shared a royal governor with Massachusetts before finally getting its own. New Hampshire sometimes had boundary disputes with its southern neighbor and with New York to the west.

Despite these difficult times, New Hampshire's economy grew. Portsmouth, the colonial capital, was an important harbor, and timber was a major natural resource. During the mid–1700s, Governor Benning Wentworth helped the colony grow by encouraging new towns in central New Hampshire, though political and economic power remained in the original coastal towns.

In the 1760s, New Hampshire residents did not protest British colonial policies as much as many other Americans did. In 1774, however, citizens took over the British fort at Newcastle, and the next year, New Hampshire eagerly sent troops to help Massachusetts fight the British. During the Revolution, ships from Portsmouth often attacked British vessels. New Hampshire's political leaders during the war included Josiah Bartlett, who signed the Declaration of Independence, and Matthew Thornton, the first governor under the state's constitution of 1776.

New Hampshire's first settlers arrive on the beach at Odiorne's Point in 1623.

New Jersey

Located between the Delaware River and the Atlantic Ocean, New Jersey was one of the smallest American colonies. The Lenni-Lenape (Delaware) Native Americans lived in the region when the first Europeans arrived in the 1600s. These included Dutch from New York, Swedes from Delaware, and English from New England. The Lenni-Lenape slowly lost their land to the settlers, and in 1758 Brothertown, New Jersey, became the site of the first reservation in America.

In 1664, King Charles II of England gave New York, New Jersey, and other American lands to his brother, the Duke of York. The duke then gave New Jersey to two friends, creating two separate Jersey colonies.

This seal was used by East Jersey when the area was a British colony. Below ears of corn, it reads "Its God Giveth Increase."

Many Quakers settled in West Jersey, while Scottish Presbyterians and English Anglicans moved to East Jersey. The colonies also included Irish and German settlers. In 1702, the two Jerseys were united and the English government took control of the colony. At the time, New York's governor ruled over New Jersey. The colony received its own governor in 1738.

During the 18th century, New Jersey was a center of American agriculture, producing grains and livestock. The colony had only a few large farms and slavery was not an important part of its agriculture. Iron making was New Jersey's only major industry.

When the American Revolution began, William Franklin, Benjamin's son, was the governor of New Jersey. Under his rule, the colony had limited protests against British policies. Still, New Jersey did participate in the Continental Congresses. One of its representatives, William Livingston, became New Jersey's first governor after independence.

Located between the major cities of New York and Philadelphia, New Jersey was the site of several major battles during the American Revolution. At Trenton, on December 26, 1776, George Washington launched a successful surprise attack on enemy forces. A week later, he won another battle in Princeton. In 1778, fighting around Monmouth marked the last major campaign of the war in the north.

● *See also Trenton and Princeton, George Washington*

Newspapers

The first printing press reached the American colonies during the 1630s. The first book printed was a collection of sayings from the Bible. In general, the early colonists did not have time to write and print their own literature; most books in America came from Europe. One noted author was Anne Bradstreet of Massachusetts. She was the first published American poet. More books appeared during the 18th century, with many focused on the political events of the era.

Newspapers were more common in the colonies. The first successful paper appeared in Boston in 1704. Later, James Franklin, Benjamin's brother, published the *New England Courant* in that city. In Philadelphia, Benjamin published his own paper as well as his famous *Poor Richard's Almanack*. Most major cities had at least one weekly paper. Residents of small towns relied on these papers to find out what was happening in Great Britain and the other colonies, since they did not have their own source of news.

Newspapers carried ads and stories on current events, just as they do today. They also often printed long essays filled with opinions on colonial politics. Authors sometimes wrote using false names, as their ideas were bound to upset many readers, including British officials. Some newspapers led the attack on the Stamp Act, since that law taxed any printed material. Loyalists also had their own papers, which criticized the Patriot cause and supported British officials.

Publishers also printed short books, called pamphlets, that promoted different political ideas. The most popular pamphlet ever printed in the colonies was *Common Sense*, by Thomas Paine. This call for independence sold 150,000 copies soon after it was published in 1776.

● See also Freedom of the Press, Thomas Paine

Dated January 15, 1739, this copy of the Pennsylvania Gazette shows how newspapers looked in colonial times.

New York

In 1609, the English explorer Henry Hudson sailed up a river in New York that now bears his name. Hudson worked for a Dutch company, and the Dutch were the first Europeans to settle in New York. When they arrived, they found Algonquian tribes living along the lower Hudson River and on Long Island, while the Iroquois controlled northern and western New York.

The first settlers reached New Netherland in 1624 and set up several forts near the Hudson River. One of these, at the end of the river, was called New Amsterdam. The Dutch were interested in the fur trade, but over time they also set up farms. The early Dutch towns included other Europeans and African slaves. By 1664, the Dutch controlled most of the land in southern New York, but that year, an English force led by James, Duke of York, took over the colony. New Netherland was renamed New York, and New Amsterdam became New York City.

The English slowly took control of the colony's political and economic life, but New York remained diverse. Its citizens came from many countries and belonged to many different faiths. In 1691, New York became a royal colony – the British crown chose its governor. The residents, however, elected the members of an assembly that drafted laws for the colony.

During the 18th century, New York's border with Canada made it a strategic spot for stationing British troops. Albany was the headquarters for the British during the French and Indian War, and several battles were fought near there. Farther north, on Lake Champlain, the British built Fort Ticonderoga, the scene of one of the first major American victories during the Revolution.

Many of New York's political leaders did not embrace the Patriot cause. But the colony had its share of Patriots who protested the Stamp Act and the Quartering Act of 1765, which allowed the British to house troops in certain local buildings. Resistance to the Quartering Act led Parliament to suspend the New York assembly for a time. During the Revolution, about one-third of all the battles took place in New York, both in and around New York City, and farther north in the Hudson and Mohawk Valleys.

New York's Revolutionary leaders included Robert Livingston and John Jay, who served in the Continental Congress. Toward the end of the war and afterward, Alexander Hamilton emerged as the state's most important national politician. After the Constitution was approved in 1788, New York City was the first capital of the new U.S. government.

• See also Alexander Hamilton, John Jay, Mohawk, Other British Colonies

At left, explorer Henry Hudson arrives in the land that would become New York. More than 150 years later, New York's streets looked like they do below.

NEW YORK, NEW YORK

New York, the largest city in the United States, started out as a village on the southern tip of Manhattan Island. In 1626 the local Algonquians sold Manhattan to the Dutch for about $24. New York's location on the Hudson River and near the Atlantic Ocean made it an excellent port. By the middle of the 18th century, it was a center for commerce in the Northeast.

During the American Revolution, the British and Americans often clashed in New York and surrounding towns. British troops landed on Staten Island in the summer of 1776, and they found many Loyalists eager to help them. Some of these New Yorkers plotted to kidnap or kill George Washington, who had arrived with his troops in April.

The British defeated the Continental Army on Long Island and in Manhattan, forcing Washington over the Hudson and into New Jersey. The British controlled New York City until after the signing of the Treaty of Paris in 1783.

• • •

North Carolina

In 1585, the English started their first settlement in North America at Roanoke Island, off the coast of North Carolina. The settlement failed, but the English returned to region in the 17th century. European settlers found a number of Native American tribes there, including the Cherokee in the west, the Tuscarora in the east, and different Algonquian tribes along the coast.

North Carolina was originally part of a larger Carolina colony. The first settlers in northern Carolina came from Virginia and lived near the coast. The colony's trees provided pitch and other materials used to build ships. By the early 1700s, two Carolinas emerged as separate colonies with their own governors.

During the mid–1700s, Quakers from Pennsylvania and German and Scotch immigrants began coming to the Piedmont, the region of Carolina inbetween the Appalachian Mountains to the west and the Atlantic Coast to the east. They tended to own small farms and had few slaves. In contrast, large tobacco and rice plantations, with many slaves, dominated the economy along the Atlantic coast. In 1768, western farmers clashed with the royal governor over control of local politics.

As the Revolution approached, North Carolina's merchants along the coast began to oppose British policies. In 1776, North Carolina was the first state to instruct its representatives in Philadelphia to vote for national independence.

North Carolina's leaders included Joseph Hewes, William Hooper, and John Penn, all

North Carolina was a very rural colony. Most people lived on small farms like this one. Here, a farm wife draws water from a well to carry to the house behind her.

signers of the Declaration of Independence. When the major fighting of the War of Independence moved south, the state was the scene of an important battle in 1781, at Guilford Courthouse.

Other British Colonies

At the start of the American Revolution, Great Britain's empire stretched around the globe. The British controlled large parts of India and claimed land in the South Pacific. Closer to America, the British owned Canada, Bermuda, and several major islands in the West Indies, including Jamaica and Barbados. The British also controlled Florida, which it had won from Spain at the end of the French and Indian War.

With its colonies, Great Britain followed a policy called **mercantilism**. The colonists provided natural resources, and they were expected to buy finished products from British manufacturers. The colonies existed to strengthen the economy of Great Britain. On the other hand, the colonies received British naval protection and had a supply of cheap goods.

Canada's resources included fish and furs. In the West Indies, plantations grew sugar, which was used to make rum and molasses. The economy of the West Indies depended largely on slave labor, more so than in North America.

During the Revolution, the new U.S. government often focused on Canada and the West Indies. Some Americans hoped Canada might join them as allies, and when the war began U.S. political leaders were reluctant to invade their northern neighbor. Still, in the summer of 1775, Patriot forces attacked Canada. After a few initial victories, the Americans were driven back across the border. Canadians fought on both sides during the war, though most remained loyal to Britain. Many American Loyalists fled to Canada for safety during and after the war.

The ruins of Scaur Hill Fort, built during the colonial period, can still be seen in Bermuda.

In the West Indies, British and French naval ships fought several battles, and French forces took control of St. Kitts and a few other islands under British control. U.S. ships also patrolled the waters, looking to capture British merchant ships.

Thomas Paine

One of the strongest calls for American independence came from the pen of a colonial newcomer, Thomas Paine. Born in England in 1737, Paine arrived in Philadelphia in 1774 and quickly joined the Patriot cause.

Paine's most famous work, *Common Sense*, appeared in January 1776. To Paine, it was clear Americans had a duty to end their ties with Great Britain and form a new nation. He stirred readers' emotions with clear arguments and harsh words against King George III. *Common Sense* shocked many Loyalists, but Americans in every colony bought thousands of copies. George Washington wrote, "I find *Common Sense* is working a powerful change in the minds of men."

Thomas Paine's ideas were considered radical at first, but they soon became very popular.

Paine's next important writing was a series of essays called *The American Crisis*. Traveling with Washington's army, Paine saw that some Americans were losing faith in the war for independence. "These are the times that try men's souls," he wrote, but Paine called on the

COMMON SENSE

Here is a selection from Paine's *Common Sense* in which Paine urges Americans to make a home for freedom in the colonies:

Freedom hath been hunted round the globe. Asia and Africa have long expelled her. Europe regards her like a stranger, and England hath given her fair warning to depart. O! receive the fugitive, and prepare in time an asylum for mankind.

•••

Americans to remain strong and keep fighting. "Tyranny, like Hell," he continued, "is not easily conquered."

Paine continued to write during the war, and he also served as the secretary for the Committee of Foreign Affairs in Congress. He later called for a new government to replace the weak one created by the Articles of Confederation. In 1787, Paine returned to Europe, and he eventually settled in France. Paine supported the French Revolution and briefly served in the government there. His later writings were too radical for most educated people of the era – even his old supporters in the United States. Paine returned to the United States in 1802 and died in poverty seven years later in New York.

Parliament

Almost one hundred years before the American Revolution, England had a bloodless "Glorious Revolution." In 1688, leading English nobles invited the Dutch Protestant William of Orange and his wife Mary to become king and queen. They replaced the Catholic king, James II, who was also Mary's father. As part of this arrangement, the new rulers agreed to give Parliament control of the English government.

Parliament was made up of the House of Commons and the House of Lords. Members were elected to the House of Commons, while the nobility had a right to sit in the House of Lords that passed from one generation to the next. All new laws were introduced in the House of Commons. The head of the government, the prime minister, came from the political party that controlled the Commons.

After the French and Indian War, Parliament worked with King George III and his advisors to strengthen Britain's control of America. In 1764, Prime Minister George Grenville called for the first new tax on Americans, the Sugar Act. Other taxes followed. By 1770, George had won greater control of Parliament, relying largely on bribes. He and his advisors then played a major role in shaping policies with the colonies.

During the Revolutionary era, some members of Parliament supported the Americans. In 1765, William Pitt welcomed American resistance to the Stamp Act. Later, Edmund Burke called for a way to keep the colonies under British rule while still guaranteeing American liberty.

After the British defeat at Yorktown in 1781, Parliament voted to end the war, ignoring George III's wish to keep fighting. After this vote, Parliament reasserted its old right to rule, weakening George's authority.

● *See also British Army, King George III, Yorktown*

Great Britain's Parliament still meets in this landmark building in London.

Pennsylvania

Located between New York and the southern colonies, Pennsylvania played an important role during the American Revolution. Its capital, Philadelphia, was the largest city in colonial America, and Congress met there during most of the Revolution.

Both Algonquians and Iroquois lived in the region before Europeans came. The largest tribes included the Lenni-Lenape (Delaware), Shawnee, Susquehannock, and Nanticoke. In 1643, a group of Swedes started the first European settlement. They were followed by the Dutch and then the English. In 1681, King Charles II of England gave control of the region to William Penn, who named the new colony. For a time, Delaware was also part of Pennsylvania.

Unlike many English settlers in America, Penn established good relations with the Native Americans, though later Pennsylvanians did clash with Native Americans on the frontier. Penn, a Quaker, also established religious freedom, and he encouraged German,

Swiss, Scottish, and other immigrants to settle there. Promoting his colony, Penn wrote that "the air is sweet and clear, the heavens serene." Although Quakers opposed slavery, the colony did have a small number of African slaves.

The Germans were the largest immigrant group, and they moved west, away from the coast. The Pennsylvania region was settled by Germans seeking religious freedom. Pennsylvania's German immigrants introduced

William Penn (left hand extended) helped create good relations with Native American in his colony.

the long, or "Pennsylvania," rifle and developed a new kind of wagon, the Conestoga.

Pennsylvania's settlers found excellent farmland and a series of rivers that made it easy to transport goods. Farmers produced large amounts of hay, grain, and livestock. The colony's first industries included ironworks, glass making, and shipbuilding. Philadelphia, with a fine harbor, was the colony's commercial heart. During the mid-18th century, wealthy merchants helped turn Philadelphia into America's center for arts and sciences.

During the Revolutionary era, Pennsylvania produced many key political figures. Boston native Benjamin Franklin spent much of his life in Philadelphia, and he represented the colony at the Second Continental Congress. John Dickinson was an early opponent of British taxes, although he did not support the Declaration of Independence. That document, as well as the U.S. Constitution, were written in Philadelphia. Pennsylvania's own state constitution, written in 1776, was the most democratic among the former colonies.

Once the Revolution began, Pennsylvania supplied large numbers of troops and important military supplies. Robert Morris, a Philadelphia merchant, helped the new American government raise money for the war.

• *See also Freedom of Religion, Philadelphia, Quakers*

WILLIAM PENN

A devout Quaker, William Penn saw his American colony as a "holy experiment." He welcomed settlers from all faiths-especially if they faced harsh restrictions in Europe. He also insisted on paying Native Americans for their lands, instead of pushing them off at the point of a gun.

Penn was born in England in 1644. He received the land that became Pennsylvania as payment for debts King Charles II owed his father. Penn only spent about five years in his colony, but he shaped its government. By 1701, Pennsylvania's elected assembly had the sole right to pass laws and raise taxes. Under Penn, the colony became a center for Quakerism. This Protestant faith opposed slavery and war and encouraged hard work.

After Penn's death in 1718, his family kept control of Pennsylvania until 1776.

• • •

Philadelphia

Founded in 1682, Philadelphia sits where the Delaware and Schuylkill Rivers meet, about 100 miles from the Atlantic Ocean. William Penn chose this spot across from New Jersey for the capital of his colony, Pennsylvania. Philadelphia turned into one of the most important cities in colonial America, famous for its culture and wealth. Like the colony as a whole, Philadelphia was dominated at first by Quakers from the British Isles, but Germans and other immigrants soon arrived and helped shape the city's commerce and social diversity.

Philadelphia had America's first public fire truck, purchased in 1719, and the first public hospital. The city's most famous resident, Benjamin Franklin, helped start America's first public library and first volunteer fire department. By the American Revolution, Philadelphia was one of the most advanced cities in the British Empire. With a population of about 35,000 it was the second-largest English city after London.

Philadelphia is closely associated with some of the most important events in U.S. history. The First Continental Congress met in the city's Carpenters' Hall in 1774. The next year, Congress met at the State House, now called Independence Hall, where the Declaration of Independence was signed. On July 8, 1776, Philadelphians were the first to hear the Declaration read in public. The city's Liberty Bell rang to call them out for this historic event. Congress met in Philadelphia

Philadelphia was the biggest and most modern city in America during the Revolutionary period.

for most of the war, except when it was held by the British during part of 1777 and 1778.

In 1787, U.S. political leaders returned to Philadelphia to draft the Constitutional Convention. The city served as the U.S. capital from 1790 to 1800.

● *See also Continental Congresses, Declaration of Independence, Pennsylvania.*

Eliza Pinckney

Eliza Lucas Pinckney may have been the most successful businesswoman in colonial America. Her efforts made indigo, the source of a popular blue dye, the second-most important crop in South Carolina. Pinckney was also the mother of two prominent Revolutionary Era leaders.

Elizabeth Lucas was born in 1722 on the Caribbean island of Antigua. Educated in England, she studied music, French, and other subjects wealthy young women of the era traditionally learned before they married. Lucas also had a strong interest in botany – the study of plants. At 16, she moved with her family to South Carolina. She was soon running her father's plantations after he returned to Antigua to serve as lieutenant governor.

In 1741, Lucas received different kinds of indigo seeds from her father and tried growing them on the plantations. At the time, most New World indigo came from French islands in the West Indies. With the help of African American slaves familiar with the crop, Lucas was able to grow indigo and turn it into a dye. Indigo production in South Carolina soon soared. Indigo gave the colony another important crop to sell abroad, along with rice.

Lucas wrote many letters and copied them into a book. Today, these letters provide useful facts about life on a Southern plantation and the activities of a colonial businesswoman. In one letter from 1742, Lucas wrote "I am so busy…I hardly allow myself time to eat or sleep…"

In 1744, Lucas married Charles Pinckney, the same year she shipped her first indigo to Great Britain. After her husband's death in 1758, Pinckney ran the family's plantations while raising her children. Her sons Thomas and Charles fought during the Revolution and were active in South Carolina politics during and after the war. In 1787, Charles represented South Carolina at the Constitutional Convention, and both brothers later served as U.S. diplomats.

British raids during the Revolution destroyed some of Pinckney's lands, so

This doll of Eliza Pinckney shows her wearing a skirt with a wide bustle in the style of the time.

she moved to her daughter Harriott's plantation and lived with her until her death in 1793. At Pinckney's funeral, George Washington asked to help carry her casket, a sign of his respect for her and her family.

- *See also Farming and Fishing, Slavery, South Carolina*

Plymouth

The Pilgrims, the first English settlers in New England, founded their colony of Plymouth on the remains of an old Native American village in Massachusetts. The settlers were actually heading for Virginia, but in December 1620, they came ashore far north of their destination. Led by William Bradford, the Pilgrims drafted an agreement, or compact, while they were still on board their ship, the Mayflower. The settlers said they would "submit to such government and governors as we should by common consent choose." This Mayflower Compact remained in force at Plymouth until 1691.

Once on land, the Pilgrims began building shelter and looking for food. During the first winter, about half of the settlers died from disease and the harsh conditions. In the spring, the remaining Pilgrims met a Patuxet Indian named Tisquantum, or Squanto. The Pilgrims were surprised to hear him speak English. In 1614, Squanto had been captured by an English sea captain and sold as a slave in Spain. He later escaped to England then returned to North America.

Squanto showed the English how to raise local crops and where to fish. He also helped the Pilgrims communicate with Massasoit, chief of the region's major tribe, the Wampanoag. For many years, the Wampanoag and the English lived together in peace. Over time, however, as the English took more Native American land, relations soured. In 1675, the two sides fought King Philip's War.

By 1650, Plymouth had about 1,000 residents. The colony included other villages near the original town. By then, a much larger group of English settlers had founded the Massachusetts Bay Colony in Boston. In 1691, Plymouth lost its independence and became part of that colony.

● See also Massachusetts, Puritans and Pilgrims

In modern-day Plymouth, a historical park shows off reconstructed homes. Visitors can imagine themselves back in early colonial times.

Pocahontas

Pocahontas was the daughter of Wahunsonacock, leader of a Native American confederacy of the same name. She was born about 1595, and lived near Jamestown, Virginia, the first permanent English settlement in North America,

Pocahontas is most famous for her heroics in an incident that may not have happened. According to John Smith, leader of the Jamestown colony, Pocahontas saved his life. Wahunsonacock had taken Smith prisoner near the end of 1607, and the chief was going to kill the Englishman.

Pocahontas stepped forward and begged her father to spare Smith. Historians doubt the story. In Smith's first written account of his captivity, he does not mention Pocahontas and her actions. He first told this story years later, in a book that mentioned several other occasions when he was supposedly rescued by young women.

After Smith's release, relations between the Wahunsonacock and English improved, until Smith began demanding corn from the Native Americans. War erupted, and in 1613 Pocahontas was kidnapped by the Virginians and held for ransom. Wahunsonacock released his prisoners,

as the settlers demanded, but the English refused to release Pocahontas. During her stay in Jamestown, she learned about English culture and converted to Christianity, taking the name Rebecca. In 1614, the chief finally agreed to end the war so he could see his daughter again.

During her captivity, Pocahontas had fallen in love with John Rolfe, the English settler who introduced tobacco farming in Virginia. The two were married soon after peace was declared. Virginia's leaders approved the marriage, hoping it would help keep the peace with the local Native Americans.

Two years later, Pocahontas, Rolfe, and their son traveled to England. The educated and refined "savage" met many influential people, including the king. In 1617, on the voyage back to Virginia, Pocahontas caught smallpox and died. She was buried in England, and her son lived there for 18 years.

- See also Jamestown, Powhatan Confederacy, John Smith, Virginia.

Pocahontas posed for a portrait with her son by a Virginia farmer. She later traveled to England and saw a world far from her childhood in America.

Pontiac

A chief of the Ottawa Indians, Pontiac was born about 1720. He led a major war against the British in the Northwest, the territory near the Great Lakes and the Ohio River Valley.

As the French and Indian War came to an end in North America, France's former Native American allies assumed they could get along with the British. But Lord Jeffrey Amherst, the British commander, refused to help the Indians as the French had. Adding to the native's concerns, American settlers were moving west and taking their lands.

In 1762, Pontiac began calling for the various Northwest tribes to fight together against the British and Americans. Aiding Pontiac was Neolin, a Delaware Indian who claimed to speak with spirits. The Prophet, as Neolin was called, said the tribes had a religious duty to unite against the Europeans so they could live as they had in past. Stirred by this message, many tribes joined Pontiac's effort, including the Chippewa, Huron, Seneca, Kickapoo, and Mingo. The war the Native Americans launched was later called Pontiac's Rebellion.

In May 1763, Pontiac led an Ottawa assault on Detroit, while his allies successfully attacked other forts and settlements. By winter, however, the Native American alliance started to fall apart. The British spread smallpox among some of the tribes, killing many Native Americans, and Pontiac realized that France was not going to provide any aid. Although some fighting continued, the war basically ended in 1764, and Pontiac made peace with the British in 1766. Three years later, he was assassinated while living in Illinois. Despite his loss to the British, Pontiac inspired future Native American leaders to seek unity in their struggles against the Europeans.

● *See also French and Indian War, Metacom, Other British Colonies, Powhatan Confederacy.*

Pontiac was the leader of the Ottawa Indians, who lived in the Great Lakes region.

Powhatan Confederacy

When English settlers landed at Jamestown in 1607, they soon met Native Americans belonging to the Powhatan Confederacy. Led by Wahunsonacock, the confederacy contained about 30 different Algonquian tribes, including the Powhatan, Pamunkey, and Kiskiack. About 13,000 people lived in the confederacy along the western rivers that emptied into Chesapeake Bay. Wahunsonacock, called Powhatan by the English, had several homes in the region.

The Powhatans knew about Europeans when the Jamestown settlers arrived. Priests and slave traders from Spain had already reached North America, and the English had earlier tried to start a colony at Roanoke Island. Wahunsonacock felt threatened by the new settlers, and he led an attack on Jamestown. The English, equipped with guns and cannons, drove off the attackers. Wahunsonacock then changed his strategy and decided to help the English, realizing he could trade with them.

Relations between the confederacy and the English went well until John Smith, leader of Jamestown, began demanding corn from some Powhatan tribes. War broke out in 1609 and lasted until 1614. The kidnapping of Wahunsonacock's daughter, Pocahontas, finally convinced the chief to end the war.

In 1622, a new Powhatan leader, Openchancanough, realized the confederacy could soon lose all its lands to the English. The Powhatans attacked again, and hundreds of settlers were killed. The English retaliated by destroying Native American crops and villages.

Wahunsonacock's daughter Pocahontas supposedly saved the life of Englishman John Smith, leader of the Jamestown, Virginia, colony.

In one battle in 1625, about 1,000 Pamunkeys were killed. The war lasted until 1632. Twelve years later, Openchancanough tried one more time to drive off the English, but now the Powhatans were outnumbered. The aging chief was captured and killed, and the Powhatan Confederacy dissolved.

● *See also Jamestown, Pocahontas, John Smith*

Puritans and Pilgrams

Although the first English setters to reach Massachusetts are often called Pilgrims, most of them called themselves Separatists. They shared ideas with a larger group, the Puritans. Their religion, a form of Protestantism, defined their values and gave them their name. Seeking to practice their faith as they chose led them to sail for North America in 1620.

Starting in the 1560s, some English Protestants wanted to purify, or reform, the national church in England. Under Henry VIII, the English had broken away from the Roman Catholic Church, but the Church of England that replaced it followed some of the old ways. The reformers, or Puritans, wanted a national church that followed the ideas of John Calvin, a French religious thinker. Among other things, the Puritans believed that God chose people to go to heaven after they died. The Puritans also said that Christians did not need a priest or minister to help them live a moral life.

All the teachings they needed came from the Bible.

Not all Puritans had the same beliefs. Some favored keeping a national church. Others, called Congregationalists, thought each local church, or congregation, should run its own affairs. But most Puritans were willing to keep some sort of national structure and work within the system of the day. The Separatists, however, went one step further: they separated completely from the Church of England to pursue their beliefs.

In 1608, a group of Separatists left England to live

Worshipping at church was the key community activity of the first English settlers in New England. They had left England for a free place to practice their faith.

in the Netherlands. Twelve years later, some of these Separatists joined others from England and sailed for Massachusetts on the *Mayflower*. Some non-Separatists also made the trip, and the entire group of about 100 people is known as the Pilgrims.

The *Mayflower* reached Plymouth in December 1620. Before landing, William Bradford, the Separatist leader, had the men sign an agreement, or compact, that outlined how they would govern the new colony. This Mayflower Compact guaranteed that all the settlers would follow the rules created by their new government, which would be based on Separatist beliefs.

Although the Separatists were the first Puritans in North America, they were soon joined by a larger group. In 1630, a large group of Congregationalists arrived in Boston. Unlike the Pilgrims, these Puritans had strong financial support from England, and they were officially known as the Massachusetts Bay Company. The new settlers hoped their moral lifestyle would inspire the Church of England to adopt their religious beliefs.

By the end of the 1600s, Plymouth had become part of the larger Massachusetts Bay colony. Congregationalists also controlled the colony of Connecticut and other parts of New England. Wherever they ruled, the Puritans refused to allow other religious groups

LEAVING FOR AMERICA

In *History of Plimoth Plantation*, William Bradford describes the Separatists' feelings as they prepared to go to North America aboard the *Mayflower* (above):

Their ends were good...their calling lawful and urgent, and therefore they might expect the blessing of God in their proceeding. Yea, though they [could] lose their lives in this action...their endeavors would be honorable.

•••

to openly practice their faith. Along with their strict religious views, the Puritans also promoted hard work and education. Their values also shaped the idea of local control in politics and the importance of individual beliefs. The Pilgrim and Puritan influence is still felt today in the United States.

• *See also Freedom of Religion, Massachusetts, Plymouth*

John Cotton was a leader of the Puritan Congregational community, which later became a force in Massachusetts and other parts of New England.

Quakers

The Society of Friends was one of several new Protestant religions that developed in England during the 17th century. Its members were nicknamed Quakers, after the group's founder, George Fox, told a judge he should tremble before God. During their services, the Quakers sat quietly, unless they were moved to speak by what they called "the Inner Light." Quakers did not believe in baptism or using ministers. Like the Puritans, Quakers valued hard work and simplicity. Unlike the Puritans, however, Quakers did not believe in a strict interpretation of the Bible.

In England, Quakers could not freely practice their religion, so many left for America. In New England, the Puritans opposed their religious beliefs, and Quakers were often arrested. Rhode Island was the only colony in the region that welcomed Quakers. After 1682, the Quakers were centered in Pennsylvania, a colony established by one of the their

This Society of Friends meeting house in Burlington, New Jersey, was an example of the plain style of the Quaker architecture and design.

own, William Penn. Quakers also settled part of New Jersey. Wherever they lived, Quakers often became successful merchants, and in Philadelphia, they dominated the city's social and political life.

The Quakers were **pacifists**, opposing violence of any kind. During the French and Indian War, Pennsylvania's government resisted efforts to raise a militia to defend against Native American attack. The government finally relented, though Quakers did not have to serve. Pennsylvania's Quakers also led the fight against slavery. In 1755, they decided together to abolish slavery among their members.

The Quakers lost their influence in Pennsylvania after the Revolution. Quakers everywhere then began to focus more on social issues, such as opposing wars, helping Native Americans, and trying to end slavery across the United States.

Quakers dressed in dark colors with little decoration on their coats or hats.

Walter Raleigh

Walter Raleigh organized the first English settlement in North America. He had a close relationship with Queen Elizabeth I, and she helped fund his efforts to start a colony on Roanoke Island, off the coast of what is now North Carolina.

Raleigh was born in England around 1554, and as a teenager he volunteered to fight with Protestant armies in France. In 1578, with his half-brother Sir Humphrey Gilbert, Raleigh organized a fleet of **privateers** – ships given government permission to attack merchant ships from other countries. Raleigh and his fleet sailed to the West Indies, but bad weather cut short the trip.

In 1584, Raleigh took over from Gilbert the plan to start an American colony. (Gilbert had died at sea while returning from North America.) Raleigh sent a ship to explore the east coast of America. The land claimed on this expedition was named Virginia, and extended north into what is now Nova Scotia. Elizabeth made Raleigh a knight for his service to the crown.

To fund another voyage to Virginia, Raleigh turned to privateering again. Queen Elizabeth also gave him money, though Raleigh had to agree to stay in England to receive it. The queen did not want to lose him, as she had lost Gilbert. In April 1585, about 100 colonists chosen by Raleigh sailed without him for Roanoke Island, joined by soldiers and scientists.

In North Carolina, the native Secotan tribe allowed the English to settle on Roanoke Island. The settlers, however, soon had problems with the Secotan and neighboring tribes, and they returned to England. In 1587, Raleigh sent over another group of colonists. The expedition's leader, John White, returned to England to recruit more settlers. When he arrived back in Roanoke in 1590, the entire colony was gone. No one knew what happened to the settlers.

Adding to Raleigh's troubles with Roanoke were some personal problems. In 1592, he angered the queen and she threw him and his wife in jail. When he was released in 1595, Raleigh led the first

Sir Walter Raleigh had a very adventurous life. He was a soldier and an explorer, and he helped found an American colony in North Carolina.

of two expeditions to South America, hoping to find gold. He failed each time. After 1603, Raleigh spent most of his time in jail as an enemy of the new king, James I. The king finally executed Raleigh in 1618.

● See also Jamestown, Roanoke, North Carolina, Virginia

Religious Freedom

When English settlers first came to North America, religion was an important part of daily life. Kings often arrested or killed subjects who defied the established, or official, religion of their realms. To many Europeans, North America offered them a place where they could worship as they chose.

For many years, however, religious freedom was not an official goal of most colonial leaders. In New England, the Puritans wanted to practice their Congregational faith, which was under attack in England. But the Puritans did not grant religious freedom to members of other churches. Quakers were especially hated; by 1661, four of them had been executed in Massachusetts, and dozens more were in prison.

Rhode Island was one exception to this religious intolerance in New England. Roger Williams, a former Puritan, founded the colony so he and his followers could worship as they chose. Williams also extended religious freedom to others. Quakers, Jews, and members of other religions not welcome elsewhere settled in Rhode Island. Outside New England, Maryland had a law that gave religious freedom to all Christians, and Pennsylvania, although ruled by Quakers, welcomed believers of other faiths.

In most of the southern colonies, Anglicanism, the established church of England, was the official religion. Members of other faiths had to pay taxes to support the established church. (This happened in New England as well.) By the middle of the 18th century, however, leaders in most colonies did not enforce all the laws restricting the rights of people who did not belong to the established churches.

Calls to weaken the power of established churches and ensure religious freedom increased after the Great Awakening. This religious movement spread through the colonies during the 1740s and 1750s. Ministers such as Jonathan Edwards and George Whitefield called for

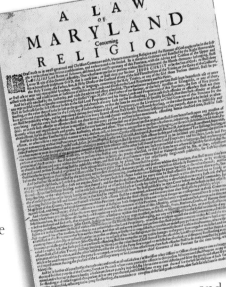

This document is the Religious Toleration Act passed by the colony of Maryland.

Protestants to renew their faith in God. The Great Awakening split apart some churches, as some people accepted these ideas and some did not want to change. The Great Awakening also fueled the growth of new Protestant groups, such as the Baptists and Methodists. In the early 1770s, Baptists in several colonies, particularly Massachusetts, demanded the freedom to worship as they chose. The Baptists saw a connection between the demands for political freedom from Great Britain and their call for religious freedom.

During the Revolutionary era, more Americans began to agree that religious freedom was an important American right. One supporter of this freedom was Thomas Jefferson. In 1779, he wrote a bill for the state of Virginia that prohibited an established church and guaranteed "that no man…shall otherwise suffer, on account of his religious opinions or beliefs." Religious freedom was also guaranteed in the new U.S. government formed in 1787, by the First Amendment of the Constitution.

• *See also Anglican Church, Congregational Church, Puritans and Pilgrims, Quakers*

Although America offered freedom of religion, most people were part of some Protestant denomination.

An Enlightened Era

Political leaders such as Thomas Jefferson, James Madison, and Benjamin Franklin were influenced by a European movement called the Enlightenment. By the middle of the 18th century, many educated people were turning away from traditional religions and embracing science. Human reason, the Enlightenment thinkers argued, would make a better world. One of the most important of these thinkers was a Frenchman, Jean-Jacques Rousseau (*above*). Men such as Jefferson did not always stop believing in God, but they did not believe God played an active role in human affairs. People influenced by the Enlightenment opposed established churches. They also said people had a natural right to worship God as they chose. Enlightenment thought shaped America's debate over religious freedom.

•••

Paul Revere

When British troops marched on the Massachusetts towns of Lexington and Concord in 1775, the residents along the way were ready for them, thanks to a warning they received from Paul Revere. A famous 19th century poem made a hero out of Revere, though two other messengers who rode with him – William Dawes and Samuel Prescott – were largely ignored.

Revere was born in 1735 in Boston. Like his father, he was a silversmith, and Revere's work is highly regarded today. Revere was also an artist, and his drawings of the Boston Massacre of 1770 stirred anger against the British. A leader of the local Sons of Liberty, Revere helped plan the Boston Tea Party in 1773, and he was probably one of the raiders who threw tea into the harbor. After the Tea Party, Revere rode to New York to inform Patriots there of the raid.

Later, Massachusetts chose him as the colony's official courier, and he carried important documents to the Continental Congress.

On the night of April 18, 1775, Revere made his famous midnight ride. He and Dawes left Charlestown, heading for Concord. The British planned to capture military supplies stored there. Revere alerted Minutemen in Lexington, where Prescott joined the ride. All three were stopped by British forces before they could reach Concord. Revere was briefly detained, then let go. Dawes returned to Boston. Prescott escaped and rode on to Concord. Revere went back to Lexington to warn Patriot leaders Samuel Adams and John Hancock about the British advance.

During the Revolution, Revere served in the militia, printed money for the Continental government, and made gunpowder. After the war, Revere returned to his silversmithing. He died in 1818.

● *See also Lexington and Concord, Minutemen, Sons of Liberty*

Paul Revere and other riders raced through the countryside warning the Minutemen.

Rhode Island

In 1636, Roger Williams arrived at Narragansett Bay and founded the first English settlement in Rhode Island. Williams, a minister, had been kicked out of neighboring Massachusetts for opposing the leaders there. He made sure his new colony welcomed followers of all religions, and Rhode Island eventually attracted Jews, Quakers, Baptists, and others.

When Williams and his followers arrived, the Narragansett were the largest Native American tribe in the region. Other Native Americans included the Wampanoag and Nipmuc. Williams had good relations with the tribes, but in 1675, the Narragansett joined the Wampanoags in King Philip's War. After an English victory, few Native Americans remained in Rhode Island.

The colony started as four separate towns: Providence, Portsmouth, Warwick, and Newport. They united in 1644 and received a royal charter that gave Rhode Island more local control than any other colony enjoyed.

The first Rhode Islanders farmed, raising corn, hay, and livestock. Later, many settlers turned to the sea for their wealth, and Newport became one of the most important colonial ports. The city's shippers often smuggled to avoid British laws that restricted colonial trade. In the 18th century, Newport was a center for the slave trade, and by 1760 Africans made up 15 percent of the city's population.

Roger Williams was the founder of Rhode Island. Here he is shown meeting Native Americans upon his arrival in what would become Providence.

After 1763, Rhode Island's merchants strongly united against British policies. During the war, Rhode Island general Nathanael Greene was a key U.S. commander, especially in the south. For several years, the British occupied Newport, and in 1778, the first joint effort of French and U.S. forces took place there. They lost the battle, but the British left the city in 1780.

● *See also Religious Freedom, Ships, Slavery*

Roanoke

English explorers first sailed to Roanoke Island, off North Carolina, in 1584. The next year, Sir Walter Raleigh sent over about 100 settlers–all men–to start the first English colony in North America. They traded with the local Secotan Indians and built huts, but they were not prepared for the hard work necessary to start a colony. Most of the settlers had come hoping to find silver and gold. After relations with the Secotan worsened, the settlers returned to England in 1586.

The next year, Raleigh organized another group of settlers. Their initial destination was the mainland near Chesapeake Bay, but they ended up on Roanoke. This group included women, as the colonists hoped to start families and stay in North America. Soon after their arrival, Eleanor and Ananias Dare had a daughter, Virginia. She was the first English baby born in North America.

The settlers made friends with another Native American tribe, the Croatan, and rebuilt the houses of the first settlers. John White, the leader of the colony, went back to England for supplies and to recruit more colonists. War between Spain and England prevented him from returning to Roanoke until 1590.

When White arrived, the colonists and Native Americans were gone. White found some words carved in a tree, but nothing explained what had happened to the settlers. Bad weather kept him from exploring a nearby island, and he returned to England. The end of the "Lost Colony" at Roanoke remains a mystery, though some local Native Americans claim the English

The first European baby born in North America was Virginia Dare. Here she is shown being baptized.

joined their tribes. Another theory suggests the settlers sailed out on small boats and were lost at sea.

• *See also Jamestown, John Smith, Sir Walter Raleigh, Virginia*

Betsy Ross

Thanks to her descendants, Betsy Ross won fame as the woman who made the first the U.S. flag. The popular story said that George Washington and two members of Congress visited her upholstery shop in 1776. Washington showed Ross the design for a flag, she made a suggestion for changing it, and soon the first "Stars and Stripes" was flying in Philadelphia. Most historians agree, however, that the Betsy Ross story is a legend.

Elizabeth Griscom Ross was a real person, and she probably made flags, but not the first U.S. flag. She was born in 1752, and when the Revolution began she ran a Philadelphia upholstery shop with her husband John. Mr. Ross died in 1776, and Ross's second husband was captured by the British during the war, leaving her a widow with two children to raise.

During the 18th century, upholsterers sewed many things, including clothes and flags. Documents from 1779 suggest that Ross made flags for Pennsylvania ships, but no one has found proof that she made the first U.S. flag. Congress did not mention making a national flag until 1777 – a year after Washington supposedly visited Ross's shop. Congress wanted the flag to have 13 red and white stripes and 13 stars on a blue background. These features appeared on a number of different flags. On the so-called "Betsy Ross flag," the stars had five points and were arranged in a circle.

Some historians suggest that Francis Hopkinson may have helped design the first U.S. flag. Hopkinson, a member of Congress from Pennsylvania, was also an artist who helped design seals for several organizations.

Whether she actually sewed the first flag or not, Betsy Ross's work on the Stars and Stripes has become part of the legend of the nation's founding.

Benjamin Rush

A renowned doctor and scientist, Benjamin Rush was also a dedicated Patriot. Born in Pennsylvania in 1746, Rush studied medicine in Scotland, then settled in Philadelphia. Concerned with politics as well as science, Rush wrote in 1769, "All the pleasures of riches, science, virtue, and even religion itself derive their value from liberty alone."

In 1775, Rush volunteered to serve in the military, and later he was named a surgeon general for the Continental Army. He represented Pennsylvania at the Second Continental Congress and signed the Declaration of Independence. Despite his loyalty to the American cause, Rush did not think George Washington should lead the military. The surgeon urged Congress to replace Washington as commander-in-chief. Rush resigned his military position in 1778, after Washington learned about his disloyalty.

Rush returned to his duties as a doctor and teacher, eventually teaching more than 3,000 students in medicine and chemistry. He wrote often on medical issues, making him the best-known doctor in the United States. He urged people not to drink and smoke, and he promoted the study of veterinary medicine. During a yellow fever epidemic that swept through Philadelphia in 1793, Rush stayed in the city to treat the sick and later wrote about the disease.

Rush also devoted himself to social reform. In 1786, he opened America's first free medical clinic. Later he also called for better treatment of prisoners and inmates of insane asylums, and he led an early anti-slavery organization.

In 1787, Rush re-entered politics. A supporter of the Constitution, he attended the Pennsylvania convention that approved that document. Rush's medical theories were sometimes wrong – he believed in bloodletting, or making patients bleed, to cure many illnesses. But Rush had a genuine desire to help the sick, improve

Benjamin Rush's first career was medicine, but he contributed to the young American nation in many different ways.

society, and defend political liberty. He died in Philadelphia in 1813.

● *See also Medicine, Slavery*

Salem Witch Trials

To many 17th century colonists, witches were humans who served Satan, harming their enemies with magical spells. In New England, Puritan leaders such as Increase Mather and his son Cotton stirred the fear of witchcraft. Several times during the century, witch "scares" broke out in New England, where supposed victims of witchcraft named neighbors as witches. Convicted witches faced imprisonment or execution.

The worst case of witch trials and executions took place in 1692 in Salem, Massachusetts. After a few girls began acting strangely, they claimed some local women were witches who had cast spells on them. Over several months, the girls accused more people of being witches, and other Salem residents also made accusations. The accused witches were usually women who did not have a high social position, though a few men were also accused.

Salem had a series of trials, where a few people did confess to being witches. Most of the accused, however, asserted their innocence. Nineteen people were hanged after being convicted of practicing witchcraft. More died in prison, and another accused was pressed to death under stones for refusing to stand trial.

The witch trials drew criticism from some people because of the lack of solid evidence against the condemned. Thomas Brattle was one of these critics. In a letter he wrote, "I pray God pity us, humble us, forgive us" for the trials.

Massachusetts governor William Phips ordered that future trials be held at a court outside Salem, where proof against the accused had to be stronger. At a trial in 1693, all the remaining accused witches were found innocent. The Salem Witch Trials were the last major witch scare in America.

● *See also Massachusetts, Pilgrims and Puritans, Religious Freedom, Women's lives*

One of the trials held in Salem in the late 1600s. More than 20 people died before the trials came to an end.

Saratoga

In September and October 1777, U.S. and British forces clashed near Saratoga, in upstate New York. Led by Generals Benedict Arnold and Horatio Gates, the Americans prevented the British from taking control of the upper Hudson River Valley. The U.S. victory also convinced France to join the war against Britain.

The British commander at Saratoga was General John "Gentleman Johnny" Burgoyne, a boastful officer without much experience leading troops. In June 1777, he left Canada with about 10,000 men and headed into New York. His forces included Canadian volunteers, Germans, and members of the Iroquois Confederacy. In July, he quickly recaptured the fort at Ticonderoga and continued south. By August, however, he was running low on supplies, so he sent troops to raid Bennington, Vermont.

General Gates (in blue) accepts the British surrender at Saratoga, a key turning point in the Revolution.

The attack was a disaster – a sign of what lay ahead in Saratoga.

Burgoyne decided to head to Albany, counting on more British troops from New York City to meet him there. Gates, the U.S. commander in the north, marched to confront Burgoyne. The Americans had about 6,000 troops; Burgoyne now had about the same.

Gates set up camp at Bemis Heights, near Saratoga. When Burgoyne attacked on September 19, Gates wanted to stay at his fort. Arnold, however, took charge and led a force into the woods. With the help of Daniel Morgan, who commanded a company of expert riflemen, Arnold inflicted heavy losses near a spot called Freeman's Farm. A soldier who served under Arnold that day praised his courage, saying the general "was as brave a man as ever lived." By the end of the day, however, the British controlled the battlefield, after Gates refused to let Arnold send more troops into battle.

The next day, Burgoyne considered attacking again, but a letter from General Henry Clinton changed his mind. Clinton was sending more British troops, and Burgoyne decided to wait for these reinforcements. As he waited, however, the Americans fired on his advance troops almost nightly. U.S. forces also cut off his supply line to Canada. By October 7, Burgoyne did not want to wait any longer for Clinton's troops, and he attacked again.

Once more, Arnold and Morgan led the U.S. troops. Despite a leg wound, Arnold helped the Americans seize high ground overlooking the British camp. The next day, the British retreated north, leaving behind 300 wounded and sick soldiers. A week later, Burgoyne surrendered. In December, the French learned of the U.S. victory. Within

HORATIO GATES

Once a professional soldier for the British, Horatio Gates settled in Virginia in 1772 and offered his services to the Americans during the Revolution. His troops called him "Granny Gates," as his appearance reminded them of an old woman. Gates first served as an aide to George Washington and led troops at several early battles. Gates, however, always sought more power, and he welcomed the fame he won after the victory at Saratoga. (Many historians, however, give most of the credit for the victory to Arnold and Morgan.) In 1778, Gates hoped to lead an attack on Quebec, but the plan never developed. Gates later commanded troops in the south, losing badly at Camden, South Carolina.

● ● ●

two months, France and the United States had signed a treaty to promote friendship and trade between the two nations, and to fight together against the British.

● *See also Benedict Arnold, Foreign Aid, New York*

School Life

In colonial America, religion was at the heart of most education, especially in Puritan New England. Protestants settlers believed everyone should at least be able to read the Bible. Beyond that, the amount of education a person received depended on their family's income. Colleges were started as training schools for new ministers, and most were tied to the dominant religion of their founders.

Public schools for most children did not exist in every colony. These schools were most common in New England. In the Middle Colonies, churches sometimes ran schools for their members' children. In the South, students were more likely to be schooled at home by relatives or a private tutor. In some cases, a wealthy family might send their children to England or Scotland for schooling.

In 1642, Massachusetts tried to require towns to educate all their children, and larger towns to open schools that taught Latin. In most public schools, students from all grades studied together in one classroom. The younger students learned the alphabet, often using a popular textbook called the New England Primer. For the letter A, students read, "In Adam's fall we sinned all." The letter K said, "Kings should be good; not men of blood."

Older children at the schools read books and copied sentences. Discipline was strict for everyone, and teachers often beat students who misbehaved. Boys and girls studied together, though most girls only received a few years of formal schooling. Girls from wealthy families might study French, drawing, or sewing at home.

Children of several ages went to school together. They used "primers" like the one above right.

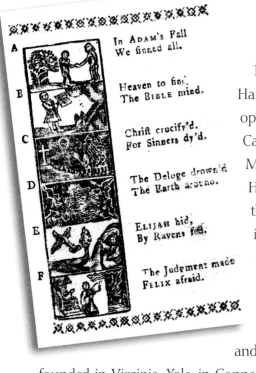

In 1636, Harvard College opened in Cambridge, Massachusetts. Harvard was the only college in the English colonies until 1693, when the College of William and Mary was founded in Virginia. Yale, in Connecticut, opened in 1701. More colleges opened in the mid-18th century. In 1752, the founders of the College of New Jersey (now Princeton) noted that schools and seminaries had a "direct tendency to advance the happiness and glory of a community" while giving students "useful knowledge and virtue." Only young men attended college, and they usually studied math, logic, grammar, philosophy, religion, Latin, and Greek. College students were much younger than they are today, usually entering school at about 15.

Young men who did not go to college often became **apprentices**. Working with older, skilled craftsmen, apprentices learned such skills as blacksmithing, shoemaking, and printing. Apprentices lived with their masters and usually worked with them for seven years. The masters were expected to teach apprentices enough reading and math skills to eventually run their own businesses.

EDUCATION FOR MINORITIES

As early as 1619, the English in Virginia planned to set up schools to teach Native Americans. The goal was to convert the Native Americans to Christianity. Overall, however, colonial leaders did not make many efforts to educate Native Americans or African Americans. A few slaves learned skills and could read, and several religious groups, such as the Quakers, opened schools for black children. Occasionally, individual slave owners taught a few of their slaves how to read and write.

•••

By the 18th century, a few towns had small public libraries, but they were not as common as today. The rich might have vast private libraries with several thousand books. In general, colonial Americans were more literate than most Europeans of the time.

● See also Family Life, Farming and Fishing.

Ships

The first European explorers and settlers of North America sailed small wooden ships across the Atlantic Ocean. The Mayflower, which arrived in Massachusetts in 1620, weighed about 180 tons and was just a little more than 100 feet long. Modern cruise ships typically displaced more than 50,000 tons of water and can be 1,000 feet long. Ships like the Mayflower

of the ship. They were useful when the wind was blowing from behind a ship on the open seas. A ship with triangular sails was called lateen-rigged. The sails ran along the length of the ship. Lateen-rigged ships were easy to turn at sea, but they were not as fast on open waters as square-rigged ships. During the colonial era, some ships combined both kinds of sails. Smaller boats used close to shore sometimes used both oars and sails.

Since most of the English colonies bordered the ocean, ships provided the major source of transportation for carrying people and goods over long distances. Smaller boats were used on rivers and lakes. Shipbuilding was an important industry along the

had to carry supplies for voyages that lasted several weeks, and there was little space for passengers and crew.

A typical ocean-going vessel had two or three masts. Sails could be either triangular or square. Square sails were flown across the width

The two ships locked in fiery battle are the English Serapis *and the American* Bonhomme Richard.

coast, especially in New England. Boston was the first major port in the colonies. New York and Philadelphia grew in the 18th century.

Early Spanish explorers and travelers to the New World came in these high-backed sailing ships known as galleons.

American shipbuilding received a boost from the Navigation Act of 1660. This law said all ships carrying British or colonial goods had to be built in the British Empire. The colonies had skilled shipbuilders and plenty of timber, along with good supplies of tar and pitch, materials used to seal ships' hulls.

In the 18th century, Chesapeake Bay shipbuilders perfected a ship called a schooner. This lateen-rigged ship could have several masts. They used smaller crews than square-rigged ships and were fast close to shore. A smaller version, with one mast, was called a sloop. American-built schooners were used for fishing and trade. They could also be armed with cannons and used for war.

When the American Revolution began, John Adams and other New Englanders saw the need for a navy.

Adams said the fleet "would contribute greatly to relief of our wants, as well as to the distress of the enemy." Before the end of the year, Congress established a Continental navy, with existing merchant ships converted to war duty. The Americans also relied on privateers to fight the British at sea. These were privately owned ships that could seize any goods found on ships they captured. American privateers took about 600 enemy ships during the war.

● *See also John Paul Jones, Plymouth, Trade, Transportation*

Slavery

Almost from the beginning, slavery played a large role in the European settlement of the New World. In the 16th century, the Spanish and Portuguese brought African slaves to South America and the Caribbean to grow sugar and coffee, and some English merchants became slave traders.

The first Africans reached colonial America in 1619, landing at Jamestown. They were certainly slaves when they arrived, but no one knows how they were treated by the people who purchased their labor. By 1640, however, most Africans reaching the colonies were slaves. Some Native Americans were also forced into slavery. Every colony had slavery, but most slaves lived in the south, growing tobacco, rice, and indigo. Some slaves also had skilled trades and lived in cities and towns.

The southern colonies developed slave codes, laws that regulated the relationship between slaves and free colonists. One law said a slave owner could not be arrested for killing a disobedient slave, "since it cannot be presumed that premeditated malice…should induce any man to destroy his own estate."

Slaves were property, bought and sold whenever a slave owner chose. Slave owners tried to keep slaves as healthy as possible without spending too much money on them. They also hired men to enforce discipline.

Some owners taught slaves how to read and write, but this was not common. The slaves tried to preserve their African customs, especially their religion, music, and folktales. Over time, slaves merged their African religions with Christian beliefs learned from their masters.

Slavery grew dramatically during the 18th century. By 1775, America had about 500,000 slaves, and they made up a large percentage of

Slaves in the American South spent many long, hard hours picking cotton for their owners.

the population in the southern colonies. During the century, slave revolts rarely broke out. One major revolt, however, took place in 1739 in South Carolina, killing about 60 people, both slaves and whites.

African Americans sometimes escaped the bonds of slavery. Some ran away. Others received their freedom from their masters. Some masters let slaves earn money at outside jobs and buy their freedom. Venture Smith of Connecticut wrote that he "paid an enormous sum for my freedom" after being sold to three different masters.

The American Revolution gave many slaves a chance to earn their freedom by fighting. Both the Patriots and

OTHER KINDS OF FORCED SERVICE

In the colonial era, many immigrants — including some Africans — came to America as indentured servants. They agreed to work for a master for up to seven years, then were free to go on their own. The servants could not travel or marry without their master's permission, and some were treated harshly. After completing their service, the servants might receive new clothes or some money.

In the 17th century, some Irish were kidnapped and forced to become indentured servants, a practice called "spiriting." In the 18th century, many Germans reached America as redemptioners. Unlike indentured servants, they did not sign a contract with their masters until reaching America. Like the servants, redemptioners served for up to seven years and had limits on their freedom.

•••

the British recruited slaves. African Americans also helped supply food to the troops, and several slaves spied for the Americans. The war also made some white Americans reconsider their support of slavery. Quakers led the call against slavery, and after the war all Northern states took steps to abolish it. But even after fighting a war for liberty, many Americans continued to accept slavery.

John Smith

A soldier and explorer, Captain John Smith made enemies wherever he went. But under his leadership, the English colony at Jamestown, Virginia, survived its first years.

Smith was born around 1580 in England. He fought in several wars in Europe, and in 1601 he served as a volunteer with Austrian forces fighting the Turks. Smith claimed he was captured and taken to Turkey as a slave, then managed to escape and return to England in 1604. Seeking new adventures, he joined a group promoting a Virginia colony.

Named to the council that would lead the colony, Smith was arrested on the voyage to North America. He was falsely accused of planning to make himself king of Virginia. The other council members finally freed Smith when they reached land. Smith continued to argue with other settlers in Virginia. At one point, he was sentenced to death for losing several men while exploring the colony. A new group of settlers freed Smith.

Smith also had trouble with the Powhatan Confederacy, the Native Americans of Virginia. While looking to trade for food, Smith and his party killed several Native Americans. The Powhatans responded by capturing him in December 1607. Smith later claimed that he would have been killed, but Pocahontas, the daughter of the Powhatan leader, saved his life. Some historians doubt this story and the details Smith gave of his earlier battles in Europe.

After they released Smith, the Powhatans and the English had good relations for about a year, and Smith led several **expeditions** to explore Chesapeake Bay and nearby rivers. In 1609, however, Smith was desperate to get corn for the colony, and he threatened a Powhatan chief, saying he would fill his ship with "dead [Powhatans]." The Powhatans then launched a war that lasted until 1614. Smith returned to England, then sailed back to America to explore New England. In 1616, he wrote a book describing that region. Smith spent the rest of his life in England, encouraging settlers to go to America. He died in 1631.

● See also Jamestown, Pocahantas, Powhatan Confederacy, Roanoke, Virginia

Captain John Smith (called Admiral in this painting) was a controversial person in early Virginia.

Sons of Liberty

After Parliament passed the Stamp Act in 1765, Americans who opposed the law flooded the streets to protest. In Boston, an angry mob stormed the home of the agent hired to collect the Stamp Act taxes. Violence spread to other colonial cities as well. The Americans who fought the tax called themselves "Sons of Liberty," taking the name from a speech made by a member of Parliament who also opposed the Stamp Act.

In the years leading up to the Revolution, the Sons of Liberty continued to organize protests against British attempts to tax Americans or deny their rights. Members often held rallies around so-called "Liberty Trees." The Sons included common laborers and important merchants. In Boston, two prominent leaders were Samuel Adams and Paul Revere. They and other Sons of Liberty planned the Boston Tea Party of 1773.

Some women joined the Patriot cause as Daughters of Liberty. To support the boycott of British goods, they used home-made cloth, called homespun, to replace fabric from overseas. The Daughters also led the efforts to convince Americans to give up tea, to protest the tax on that popular drink. In every colony, the Sons and Daughters of Liberty helped shaped the debate on America's desire for equal rights and freedom.

TEA FOR FREEDOM

In 1773, the British tea tax led the New York Sons of Liberty to issue a statement. "It is essential," they wrote, "to the freedom and security of a free people that no taxes be imposed on them but by their own consent or [that of] their representatives." They declared that as long as tea was taxed, anyone who brought tea into the colony ". . . shall be deemed an enemy to the liberties of America."

• • •

ADVERTISEMENT.

THE Members of the Affociation of the Sons of Liberty, are requefted to meet at the City-Hall, at one o'Clock, To-morrow, (being Friday) on Bufi-nefs of the utmoft Importance ;—And every other Friend to the Liberties, and Trade of America, are hereby moft cordially invited, to meet at the fame Time and Place.

The Committee of the Affociation.

Thurfday, NEW-YORK, 16th December, 1773.

This advertisement called for people to get involved in the growing Revolutionary movement.

• See also Samuel Adams, Boston Tea Party, Parliament, Paul Revere, Stamp Act

South Carolina

In the mid–16th century, the French and Spanish tried but failed to start colonies in what is now South Carolina. The Native Americans of the region included the Catawba, Cherokee, and Cusabo.

England started the first permanent colonies in the Carolinas during the 1660s. King Charles II gave a group of proprietors land, and settlers from Virginia founded what became North Carolina. In 1670, English colonists landed in South Carolina, and 10 years later they founded Charles Town (Charleston), along the Ashley and Cooper Rivers. In 1712, the two Carolinas received separate governors for the first time.

Slavery quickly took root in South Carolina, and in the early part of the 1700s, slaves outnumbered white settlers. Rice was the major crop, later followed by indigo. Charleston became a commercial center and the only major southern city in America. Merchants often traded with Native Americans in the interior of the colony, though attacks by other natives in 1715 threatened South Carolina. The settlers made peace with the invading Yamasee in 1717.

By the time of the American Revolution, South Carolina was a royal colony. A key supporter of the Revolution was Henry Laurens, a successful Charleston merchant. He later helped negotiate the Treaty of Paris. During the war, Charleston was the target of several British attacks. William Moultrie led the defense of the city in 1776. Three years later, the British returned to South Carolina, and in 1780 they captured Charleston. Fighting continued in the state, with many Loyalists battling for the British. The Americans won a major victory at the

By the mid-1700s, when this painting was made, the South Carolina port of Charleston was the major city of the South. It was a key target of the British in the war.

Battle of Cowpens in 1781, and inflicted heavy enemy losses at Eutaw Springs, one of the last battles of the war.

● *See also Francis Marion, Eliza Pinckney, Slavery, Trade*

Spanish Colonies

Starting with the voyage of Christopher Columbus in 1492, Spain supported exploration and settlement of the so-called New World. By 1565, Spain had established a colony at St. Augustine, Florida, and had tried to start settlements in the Carolinas. The Spanish also had colonies in the West. Starting in 1598, Spain built missions and forts in Arizona, New Mexico, Texas, and California. Spanish priests tried to convert Native Americans to Roman Catholicism and used the Indians as workers at their missions. Spain also brought African slaves to their North American colonies. In the southwest, Spanish ranchers called vaqueros introduced many of the methods later used by American cowboys.

During the 18th century, Spain's relations with France and Great Britain influenced events in its American colonies. A war between Spain and Great Britain in 1739 led English colonists to attack Florida, and Spain launched an invasion of Georgia in 1742. During the French and Indian War, Spain sided with France against Great Britain. After the war, Spain lost Florida to the British, but it acquired French lands west of the Mississippi River and the city of New Orleans.

Spain, unlike France, did not actively fight for the Americans during the American Revolution. The Spanish provided military aide and fought British troops where and when it served their interests. Spanish ships captured British forts in Mississippi and Florida, and Spanish troops battled the British in St. Louis.

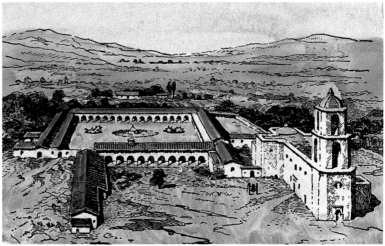

The earliest Spanish settlements in California were a series of Catholic churches called "missions."

After the war, Spanish control of the lower part of the Mississippi River made trade difficult for some U.S. farmers and merchants. The issue was finally settled in 1795, as Pinckney's Treaty gave Americans the right to sail the entire length of the river.

● *See also Foreign Aid, French and Indian War, Georgia, Other British Colonies*

Stamp Act

After Great Britain's victory in the French and Indian War, Parliament decided the American colonies had to contribute more money for their own defense. The first new taxes on the colonies appeared in the Sugar Act of 1764. The next year, Parliament passed the Stamp Act. It was the first direct British attempt to collect taxes from the Americans. The law required colonists to buy stamps for any printed materials: legal and commercial documents, newspapers, pamphlets, magazines – even playing cards.

Almost immediately, some colonists attacked the Stamp Act. John Adams said the law was "fabricated…for battering down all the rights and liberties of America." Many opponents believed the British government did not have a right to collect taxes on economic activity within America, since the colonies did not have any representatives in Parliament. Some Americans repeated the cry, "Taxation without representation is tyranny." British supporters of the tax responded by saying the Americans had "virtual" representation: members of Parliament represented all English citizens – including Americans – not just the voters who elected them.

In America, Stamp Act protests turned violent, as mobs in Boston destroyed the homes of some colonial officials. The protesters called themselves the Sons of Liberty, and similar groups carried out more violence in other cities. By the time the Stamp Act took effect in November 1765, the commissioners hired to collect the tax were too scared to do their jobs.

By then, representatives from nine colonies had met in New York and voiced their united opposition to the tax. Some members of Parliament also opposed the Stamp Act, and the law was repealed in February 1766. But British officials were ready to introduce new taxes, and the colonists were increasingly willing to oppose them.

• *See also Boston Tea Party, Intolerable Acts, Sugar Act, Taxation*

British laws forced colonists to buy stamps like these for all printed matter. Colonial opposition to such taxes helped lead to the Revolutionary War.

Sugar Act

Before and during the French and Indian War, the American colonies enjoyed the benefits of a British policy called **salutary neglect**. British officials let Americans largely ignore certain laws and taxes, especially ones regarding commerce. American rum makers, for example, avoided paying a duty, or tax, on imported molasses, the main ingredient for their product. They smuggled in the molasses, and Great Britain let them get away with it.

Salutary neglect ended in 1764, when Parliament passed the American Revenue Act. Also called the Sugar Act, the law raised or introduced duties, or taxes on traded goods. These items included sugar, coffee, and textiles. The law also limited which goods Americans could sell to foreign countries. To enforce the new law, as well as old ones, Parliament tightened its patrol of American waters. British naval ships had the power to seize goods from merchants who had not paid the taxes.

Some Americans protested the Sugar Act and the attempt to control the colonies. Massachusetts lawyer James Otis wrote that if anyone taxed him without his consent, "he deprives me of my liberty and makes me a slave." The idea that Americans could not be taxed without having

In harborside warehouses, giant rum barrels awaited shipment throughout the colonies. The taxes the British put on such goods were disliked by the colonists.

their own representatives in Parliament began to spread. Lawmakers from New York and Massachusetts said the Sugar Act violated their charters with the British government. Parliament, however, did not agree, and the next year it introduced another new tax law, the Stamp Act. The first rumblings of colonial anger stirred by the Sugar Act exploded into violence with the new tax.

● *See also Boston Tea Party, Intolerable Acts, Other British Colonies, Stamp Act, Taxation*

Taxation

Benjamin Franklin once wrote that "nothing can said to be certain, except death and taxes." The American colonists paid a number of different taxes, knowing these funds helped pay for military defense and other public services. But starting in 1764, Great Britain's attempts to introduce new taxes stirred anger in the colonies.

Within the colonies, local governments relied on a variety of taxes. Most landowners paid taxes on their property. Voters in most colonies also paid a poll tax to county or town governments. In general, English colonists paid lower taxes than they would have if they still lived in England.

The first English taxes on the colonies were duties and tariffs, forms of taxes collected on goods brought into or out of America. These duties usually applied to all British colonies, not just the ones in America.

In 1724, a British court ruled that the Crown and royal officials could not levy taxes on the colonies. Only Parliament and colonial assemblies had that right. Parliament, however, did not exercise that right for 40 years. During this period, the British lawmakers largely ignored affairs within

This group of men in London was the subject of most of the American colonists' protests. The members of Parliament passed laws that taxed Americans unfairly.

the colonies. That attitude ended after the French and Indian War, as Parliament passed the Sugar Act. Along with raising duties on several items, including sugar, the law also called for stronger methods of collecting taxes.

The Stamp Act of 1765 introduced a tax on documents used in the colonies. To the Americans, this tax was drastically different than the old duties and tariffs. Those taxes were **levied** on items leaving or entering America, that is, they were external. The Stamp Act, however, was on internal items, documents made and used within the colonies.

Since the Americans were not represented in Parliament, they had no say in this new taxation. Some colonists claimed this denied their legal rights as British citizens. "Taxation

without representation is tyranny" became a popular patriot slogan. The patriots also argued that they would never have meaningful representation in Parliament, since the colonies were so far from London. Many Americans argued that only their colonial assemblies could ever levy internal taxes.

After the protests against the Stamp Act, Parliament passed a new round of taxes in 1767 called the Townshend Revenue Act. These taxes were external, and so they should not have upset the colonists – in theory. But by now, many Americans denied Parliament's right to collect any taxes.

To protest the new duties, Boston merchants led a boycott of the taxed items. By 1770, Great Britain repealed all of the Townshend duties except for the one on tea. This tax played a part in the Boston Tea Party of 1773.

Examples of early colonial paper money. At first, each state printed its own.

By the time Thomas Jefferson wrote the Declaration of Independence in 1776, his list of complaints against King George III barely mentioned taxes. Taxation, however, sparked the resistance to Great Britain that led to the American Revolution.

• *See also Boston Tea Party, Intolerable Acts, Stamp Act, Sugar Act*

PROTESTS OF THE TOWNSHEND ACTS

In 1768, Samuel Adams called for other colonies to join Massachusetts in opposing the Townshend Acts.

"...it is an essential, unalterable right in nature, engrafted into the British constitution as a fundamental law...that what a man has honestly acquired is absolutely his own, which he may freely give, but cannot be taken from him without his consent....the acts made [in Parliament] imposing duties on the people of this province...are infringements of their natural and constitutional rights; because...those acts, grant their property without their consent."

●●●

Tools

Arriving in America from Europe, the first colonists had to bring the tools they needed to survive. Later, the settlers had time to make their own tools with resources found in the colonies. In general, the tools used in America were the same ones Europeans had used for hundreds of years.

Since the first settlers needed to clear trees for farms and cut timber for houses, their most important tool was the axe. Another cutting tool was the adz, which was shaped like a hoe. Axe heads and other cutting tools were made out of iron and the handles were made of wood. Many Native Americans used stone for their axes and other tools, though over time they traded with the settlers for metal goods.

To split wood, a settler might use a maul and froe. A maul was a short wooden club used to drive the froe, a wedge-shaped tool made of wood or iron. Other common tools included picks, shovels, and hoes. On farms, plows were usually made of wood, though the plowshare, which actually cut into the earth, could be made of iron. Settlers also imitated the local Native American tribes and used sticks or antlers for simple hoes. To cut grain, farmers used scythes, long metal blades attached to wooden handles.

Workers with special skills had their own tools for their crafts. Blacksmiths had anvils and several hammers to shape iron into different objects. Joiners used different axes, like the one above, and planes to shape wooden chairs and tables. Coopers made barrels and small wooden items using similar tools.

• See also Family Life, Farming and Fishing, Transportation, Trade.

At top is an colonial-era axe. At bottom, a worker uses a wine press to squeeze grapes.

Trade

As part of the British Empire, the American colonies had to ship natural resources to Great Britain and buy finished goods in return. This trade, as well as trade within the colonies and with the British West Indies, helped some American merchants become rich. Trade also made shipbuilding an important American industry.

Most of the shipping trade – and the wealth associated with it – was centered in the major cities of Boston, New York, Philadelphia, and Charleston. Common goods shipped overseas included tobacco, timber, materials used in shipbuilding, fish, and food. Within the colonies, merchants and farmers shipped goods by boat and wagon.

Overseas trade sometimes involved three voyages on one round trip, which is known as triangular trade. American ships might sail to the West Indies, carrying food products or lumber, then take on sugar and molasses to bring to Great Britain. The ships then carried manufactured goods from Great Britain back to America. Colonial ships also sometimes carried slaves from Africa to the West Indies or southern American colonies as part of the triangle. In general, however, most trade was direct between America and Britain or the West Indies.

Most British trade laws were designed to help British merchants and shippers. To avoid laws that restricted trade or taxed goods, some shippers turned to smuggling. Molasses and sugar from the West Indies were often smuggled into America. So was tea, during the years just before the American Revolution. Well-known smugglers included the Browns of Rhode Island and Boston's John Hancock. The British lacked the ships and custom officials to enforce its trade laws, though Parliament tried to tighten its control of trade during the late 1760s.

Trade worked both ways across the Atlantic. After delivering goods to early Virginia colonies, these ships returned with these barrels of tobacco.

- *See also Parliament, Ships, Slavery, Taxation, Transportation*

Transportation

When English settlers reached the eastern part of North America, they found rivers and trails that eased transportation. Many of the rivers were deep enough for ships to sail on them at least partway. Important rivers for transportation included the Connecticut, Hudson, Delaware, Susquehanna, Potomac, and Savannah. In French lands to the north and west, trappers and explorers used the St. Lawrence and Mississippi Rivers. On smaller rivers and streams, the settlers used small boats, including canoes, which were first used by Native Americans.

On land, the colonists relied on trails and paths that the Native Americans had used for centuries. One important trail, the Mohawk, ran through western Massachusetts into New York, out to the Great Lakes. Another major Native Americans trail was the Great Trading and War Path, which the settlers called the Great Road of the Valley. The trail ran along the Blue Ridge Mountains in Virginia and branched off into other colonies, including Pennsylvania and the Carolinas. Part of the trail became the Wilderness Road, the path Daniel Boone followed through the mountains into Kentucky.

Over time, the settlers widened some of the existing trails. They also made their own roads, though most were just simple dirt paths. Roads connecting towns were more common in the

As the nation grew, water transport on rivers and canals became more useful. This canal in New Hope, Pennsylvania, still offers rides to visitors.

north, where towns were closer together than in the south. Two early roads, opened around 1710, were the Boston Post Road and the Old Post Road. Later in the 18th century, companies built private roads and collected tolls from the people who traveled them.

As the names suggest, post roads were used primarily for the postal service, with mail carried on coaches that stopped at stations, or posts, along the way. Passengers could also pay to ride on the coaches, which were pulled by horses.

The coaches had four wheels, but some smaller horse-drawn vehicles had only two. To cross rivers, the coaches usually sailed on ferries, as building bridges was often difficult. Coaches, carriages, and horses were too expensive for most settlers. Walking was the common form of transportation for most people.

Farmers often used oxen to pull simple wagons. In the early-18th century, German immigrants in Pennsylvania introduced an improved wagon, the Conestoga.

It could safely carry more goods than other wagons. During the French and Indian War, the British military forces used Conestogas to haul supplies, and afterward settlers used them to cross the Appalachian Mountains.

The first great era of U.S. transportation began well

TRAVELING THE POST ROAD

In colonial times, a trip between Boston and New York took several days, and passengers had to stay at inns along the road (*below*). Here, a teacher named Sarah Kemble Knight describes a journey she took on horseback in 1704.

Wednesday, October 4th.—About four in the morning we set out for Kingston. The road was poorly furnished with accommodations for travelers, so that we were forced to ride 22 miles…before we could [feed] so much as our horses, which I exceedingly complained of….

Thursday, October 5th.-…About seven that evening, we came to New London ferry; here by reason of a very high wind, we met with great difficulty in getting over — the boat tossed exceedingly, and our horses capered at a surprising rate, and set us all in a fright….

•••

after the American Revolution, as governments and companies built the first paved roads and dug canals to improve shipping.

● *See also Ships, Trade*

Treaty of Paris

With the British defeat at Yorktown in October 1781, Parliament was finally ready to discuss peace with the United States. The next April, the British sent Richard Oswald to Paris to meet with Benjamin Franklin. The famed American scientist and statesman, along with John Adams and John Jay, drafted the treaty that ended the American Revolution. Henry Laurens later joined the other U.S. diplomats.

Congress had instructed its representatives to consult with French leaders, since they had joined the war against Britain. Adams and Jay, however, did not trust France and wanted to negotiate secretly with the British. Although Franklin was friendly with French leaders, he also thought the United States would do better without French involvement. He and Oswald met to construct the treaty.

The Americans had several major demands. First, they wanted the British to recognize U.S. independence and withdraw their troops. The United States also wanted its boundaries set as the Mississippi River and the Great Lakes and the right to fish off Newfoundland.

The two sides agreed on these issues, but they clashed over debts and Loyalists. The Americans finally said British merchants could try to collect money owed them since 1775. The Americans, in return, agreed to stop attacks on Loyalists and encourage the states to repay them for any property they lost during the war..

Britain and the United States reached an agreement in November 1782. The British then negotiated separate peace agreements with the

This 1784 map shows the extent of the new nation that was called the United States of America.

Americans' allies, France, Spain, and the Netherlands. The diplomats signed the Treaty of Paris in September 1783, and Congress approved a final version in May 1784.

● See also John Adams, Benjamin Franklin, John Jay, Loyalists, Yorktown.

Trenton and Princeton

By December 1776, the British had won several major battles in and around New York City, forcing General George Washington to retreat through New Jersey into Pennsylvania. Even worse for Washington, thousands of his soldiers were scheduled to go home on January 1. Hoping to win a victory before he lost most of his troops, Washington launched a bold surprise attack.

On Christmas night, Washington and his men ferried across the Delaware River through cold, sleet, and wind. At daybreak they attacked Trenton, New Jersey, where Hessians, German hired soldiers fighting for Great Britain, had just finished their holiday celebrations. The Americans stunned the Hessians, killing or wounding more than 100 and taking almost 900 prisoners before returning to Pennsylvania. One U.S. soldier later wrote, "Never were men in higher spirits than our whole army is."

After the victory, Washington promised his men extra money to stay with him six more weeks. The forces agreed, and they returned to Trenton on December 30. Meanwhile, a much larger British force under Lord Cornwallis was approaching. Fighting broke out on January 2, 1777, but as night fell, Cornwallis halted the attack. Thinking he had Washington trapped, Cornwallis planned to wait until morning to fight again.

Late that night, most of the American forces quietly left their camp, keeping fires burning to make it seem they were still there. The trick saved the Americans from Cornwallis's attack, and Washington then made his own assault on a smaller British force outside Princeton. With his daring moves, Washington had regained control of part of New Jersey. More importantly, he gave hope to Americans who had started to think they might lose their war for independence.

George Washington, with hat raised, leads his blue-coated troops in the Battle of Princeton.

United States Constitution

As Americans fought for their independence on the battlefield, they struggled to form a government to run their new country. In 1777, the Second Continental Congress drafted the Articles of Confederation, but the states did not approve it until 1781. Under the Articles, the states kept most political power. Within just a few years, however, some leaders thought the new national government was too weak. In 1783, Alexander Hamilton wrote that Congress lacked the power to "mak[e] every member of the Union contribute in just proportion to the common necessities."

Over time, more people began to see the flaws in the Articles of Confederation. In the fall of 1786, some political leaders met in Annapolis, Maryland, to discuss forming a new government. Then, in May 1787, leaders from every state except Rhode Island met in Philadelphia to change the Articles of Confederation. The delegates included George Washington, James Madison, Benjamin Franklin, and George Mason. Washington was a Federalist – he supported a stronger national government. He was elected president of the convention. Although he could not take part in the debates, the other delegates knew how he felt and respected his opinion. "Be assured," wrote James Monroe of Virginia, "his influence carried the government."

Madison had led the call for the Constitutional Convention, and he played a large role in shaping the new government that emerged. His "Virginia Plan" called for a government with three branches. The legislature (Congress) would have two separate houses, with representatives sent by the states. This branch would make laws and have the power to collect taxes. The executive branch would carry out these laws. The third branch was the judiciary. Its judges would make sure the laws were carried out fairly.

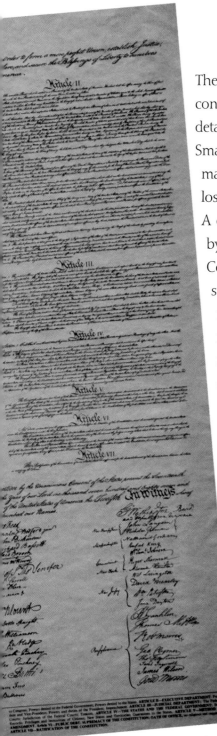

The delegates at the convention debated the details of Madison's plan. Small states wanted to make sure they did not lose power to larger ones. A compromise, suggested by Roger Sherman of Connecticut, let each state have an equal number of representatives in the Senate. In the House of Representatives, the number of representatives would be based on a state's population. The delegates also debated slavery. They finally agreed to end the slave trade – but not slavery itself – in 1808. Slaves, meanwhile, would be counted as 3/5 of a person when figuring a state's population.

THE BILL OF RIGHTS

Many Anti-Federalists demanded that Congress add a bill of rights to the Constitution. Many states had a bill of rights, guaranteeing such things as free speech, freedom of religion, and the right to a fair trial. In 1789, James Madison proposed a series of amendments to the Constitution. Congress approved 12 of these, and the states ratified 10. These first 10 amendments form the U.S. Bill of Rights. Today, the Constitution has 16 amendments in addition to the Bill of Rights.

•••

On September 17, 1787, 39 delegates signed the Constitution. They represented 11 of the 13 states. (Alexander Hamilton of New York also signed, but he was not officially representing his state). The states then held conventions to decide whether or not to ratify the document. In some states, the vote was close, as Anti-Federalists – opponents of strong federal government – tried to defeat it. By June 1788, 11 states had approved the document, and the new U.S. government began in April 1789.

● *See also Articles of Confederation, Continental Congresses, Declaration of Independence, Alexander Hamilton, James Madison, Philadelphia.*

U.S. CONSTITUTION

Valley Forge

As the winter of 1777–78 approached, George Washington set up his headquarters at Valley Forge, Pennsylvania. During the year, the British had won major battles at Brandywine and Germantown and captured the American capital of Philadelphia. Even after these losses, however, most of the U.S. troops still supported Washington and the war.

Reaching Valley Forge, many of the soldiers were shoeless and wearing rags. Food was scarce, although American farmers had produced a large harvest that fall. Washington's problem was getting the food and supplies he needed from Congress. In a letter to Henry Laurens, president of Congress, Washington wrote, "No man, in my opinion, ever had his measures more impeded than I have, by every department of the Army."

The soldiers took almost a month to build their huts. In the meantime, many shivered in crude shelters, often without blankets. Luckily, the winter was not as harsh as others during the Revolution. To help ease the starving, Washington sent troops into New Jersey and Delaware to look for food. As the winter went on, the soldiers often chanted, "No pay, no clothes, no provisions, no rum." Despite the miserable conditions, few of the men deserted – a sign of their dedication to their commander and their cause. Illness and hunger, however,

At Valley Forge today, visitors can see buildings modeled on the ones that the American army used.

killed about 2,500 of the 10,000 troops stationed at Valley Forge.

Along with his supply problems, Washington faced growing criticism in Congress over his leadership. Some representatives wanted to replace him, and General Horatio Gates seemed ready to take the job. Another of Washington's enemies was General Francis Conway, an Irish volunteer. The rumblings against Washington are known as the Conway Cabal. Most of the officers, however, remained loyal to Washington.

One of Washington's most faithful supporters was the Marquis de Lafayette. At Valley Forge, the young French nobleman impressed the American troops when he did not ask for special treatment. Another foreign officer, Baron Friedrich von Steuben, played an important role during the difficult winter.

Von Steuben trained the Americans using methods he learned in his homeland of Prussia.

He also encouraged the U.S. officers to show more concern for the soldiers, to earn their loyalty.

Slowly the situation at Valley Forge began to brighten. General Nathanael Greene took over as the supply officer and greatly improved the flow of food and other goods. Congress took steps to improve recruiting and the selection of officers. And thanks to von Steuben, the Continental Army was more professional than ever before.

By the end of April, Washington learned that the French had agreed to join the war against Great Britain. The winter at Valley Forge had not been easy, but the Americans were a now stronger force, and they were ready to continue the war.

• See also Foreign Generals, Lafayette, George Washington

Washington, on the right, Von Steuben, and freezing soldiers at Valley Forge. The conditions were harsh in the camp, but most men survived.

A SOLDIER'S STORY

Albigence Waldo, a military doctor from Connecticut, kept a diary during the winter of 1777. Here is some of what he wrote:

The army, which has been surprisingly healthy [before], now begins to grow sickly from this campaign . . . . I am sick, discontented, and out of humour. Poor food — hard lodging — cold weather— fatigue — nasty clothes — nasty cookery — vomit half the time— . . . . I can't endure it. Why are we sent here to starve and freeze? It's all confusion and cold and hunger — a pox on my bad luck!

• • •

Virginia

The largest of the thirteen English colonies, Virginia was also the first one settled. The original land claim stretched from Maine to Florida, but over time, other colonies were carved out of this area.

The first settlers reached Jamestown, along the Chesapeake Bay, in 1607. During their first few years, the English, led by John Smith, sometimes clashed with the Powhatan Confederacy, a union of Algonquian tribes led by a chief also called Powhatan. The growing English population finally defeated the Native Americans in 1644, killing them all or pushing them westward.

The economy of Virginia was based on growing tobacco, which John Rolfe introduced to the colony in 1612. The large plantations needed workers, and farmers acquired both indentured servants and African slaves to grow the crop. The first Africans reached Jamestown in 1619, probably as indentured servants. By the end of the century, thousands of slaves lived in Virginia, and their numbers grew dramatically. By the time of the American Revolution, the colony had about 200,000 slaves out of a total population of 500,000.

To encourage settlers to come to Virginia, its leaders offered free land. In 1656, John Hammond published a pamphlet promoting Virginia's strong points. "I affirm the country," he wrote, "to be wholesome, healthy and fruitful." In reality, disease was common at the time, and often deadly. Virginia's population would not have grown without the new settlers seeking their fortune.

In 1619, Virginia started the first elected assembly in English North America, the House of Burgesses. After 1624, the colony had a governor appointed by the crown. During the Revolutionary Era, the governors and the Burgesses sometimes fought over the issues of the day, such as the Stamp Act and the Townshend Acts.

Anglicanism was the colony's official religion, but over time members of other churches were found in the colony, including Presbyterians, Baptists, and other Protestants. Virginia politics

and society were controlled by wealthy planters, who often copied the latest styles from England.

During the French and Indian War, Virginia troops fought along the western frontier. The war gave a young Virginian named George Washington his first military experience. After the war, the British tried to force the Americans to pay more taxes. Several Virginia politicians led the protests against these efforts. One outspoken Patriot was Patrick Henry. In 1775, he supposedly made his famous cry, "Give me liberty or give me death!" Other leaders from Virginia included Thomas Jefferson, George Mason, and Richard Henry Lee. In June 1776, at the Second Continental Congress, Lee introduced the resolution of declaring independence.

Visitors can tour this colonial-era Philip Randolph House in Williamsburg, Virginia.

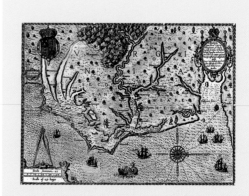

An Important First

In June 1776, Virginia (*map above*) became the first state to issue a declaration of rights. Written by George Mason, the document said "all power is vested in... the people" and that political leaders were the people's "servants." The Virginia Declaration of Rights guaranteed freedom of the press and religion, as well as other rights. It influenced the Bill of Rights, the first 10 amendments to the Constitution.

•••

After the war began, Virginia's governor, Lord Dunmore, led several attacks that destroyed the towns of Hampton and Norfolk. Patriot forces then drove him from the state. In 1779, the British launched naval raids on the state, and fierce fighting continued in Virginia until the U.S. victory at Yorktown in 1781.

● *See also Anglican Church, Patrick Henry, Jamestown, Thomas Jefferson, Roanoke, George Washington, Yorktown*

George Washington

"George Washington once wrote, "I have no wish superior to that of promoting the happiness and welfare of this country." During a lifetime of military and government service, Washington did as much as anyone to create the United States of America and guarantee its survival.

The son of a Virginia farmer, Washington was born in 1732. At the age of 20, he was appointed a major in the Virginia militia. In 1754, he led troops against the French, in what has sometimes been called the first battle of the French and Indian War. At 23, Washington was named commander of the Virginia militia and was put in charge of the colony's defense.

In 1758 Washington resigned his military position to return to private life. In 1759, he married Martha Custis, a wealthy widow with two children. Her fortune made Washington one of the wealthiest men in Virginia. Over the years, however, Washington often struggled to pay his debts as he ran his plantation at Mount Vernon.

Washington entered Virginia politics, serving in the House of Burgesses. After 1765, Washington opposed the Stamp Act and other British measures that restricted freedom in the American colonies. He urged the colonists to defend their rights, even as it became clear that resisting the British would lead to war.

In June 1775, after American and British forces fought at Lexington and Concord, the Second Continental Congress named Washington commander in chief of the new Continental Army. He was a logical choice, since he had shown his bravery and leadership skills during the French and Indian War, and he was a strong supporter of the patriot cause.

Serving without pay, Washington was soon leading U.S. forces already fighting outside Boston. When he took command, Washington thought the American soldiers lacked discipline, and the enlisted men from New England were "an exceeding dirty and nasty people."

Throughout the war, Washington tried to turn his forces into a

George Washington was perhaps the most important American during the revolution. The Virginia native was a military and political leader around whom Americans rallied.

Washington's home at Mt. Vernon, Virginia, remains a popular tourist destination.

KING GEORGE 1?

In 1782, several of George Washington's officers made a startling suggestion. They wanted him to become the first king of the United States. Washington was appalled at the idea and quickly rejected it. He had been fighting to end the kind of total power kings enjoyed over their citizens. Before leaving his command, Washington also ended a plan by some of his officers to keep the army together after the war. The officers hoped to threaten Congress and force it to raise the money soldiers were owed for their military service.

•••

professional army capable of at least holding off the British, if not beating them at every battle.

After the British left the city, Washington marched his troops to New York. The British won a series of victories there. At the end of 1776, Washington's army finally won a major battle in Trenton, New Jersey. Another at Princeton followed shortly after. These victories boosted American spirits at a time when the American Revolution seemed lost.

For most of the war, Washington faced endless problems. His small army included local militia and soldiers who were not properly trained. Washington had trouble getting supplies from the U.S. government. And at times, he faced opponents in the army and in Congress who wanted to remove him as commander in chief. Despite these struggles, Washington kept the army together long enough to defeat the British. His last major victory, at Yorktown, Virginia, ended the war.

Washington returned to political life in 1787, serving at the Constitutional Convention. His support for the Constitution helped win its approval. Washington was also chosen to serve as the first President under the new government. Washington left office in 1797 and died in 1799. Years later, Thomas Jefferson wrote that Washington was "a wise, a good, a great man."

Although not a brilliant scholar or outstanding general, Washington led by his example. He fought courageously and served his country whenever he was asked. As president, his actions served as a model for future presidents to follow.

● *See also French and Indian War, Trenton and Princeton, Valley Forge, Virginia, Yorktown*

John Winthrop

Before the Puritans left England in 1630, they elected John Winthrop as their governor. Trained as a lawyer, Winthrop was also a devout Puritan. Like many Puritans, he hoped to practice his "pure" faith while seeking his fortune in America. Winthrop wrote that the Puritan colony would be "like a city upon a hill; the eyes of all people are on us."

Winthrop was born in 1588 in Suffolk, England. In 1629, he and small group of Puritans won control of the charter for the land claimed by the Massachusetts Bay Company. Unlike the owners of most colonial charters, Winthrop and the others planned to live in and directly control Massachusetts.

Winthrop served as governor until 1634, and again in the late 1630s and 1640s. He supported a strong central government in the colony, although individual congregations of Puritans ran their own religious affairs. Winthrop kept a journal of his years in power, providing details of the early history of Massachusetts. The governor also noted some of the colony's political and religious disputes. These included his conflict with Anne Hutchinson, who believed God had spoken directly to her through the Holy Spirit. Hutchinson's ideas went against Puritan beliefs, and Winthrop led the efforts to banish her from Massachusetts.

In 1643, Winthrop organized the New England Confederation, the first union of English colonies in America. Formed for military purposes, the confederation included Plymouth, Connecticut, New Haven, and Massachusetts. Winthrop died six years later. His son John Jr. later became governor of Connecticut.

● *See also Congregational Church, Massachusetts, Plymouth, Puritans and Pilgrims, Religious Freedom*

John Winthrop greets citizens and soldiers in the new colony in Plymouth. Note the curved metal helmets worn by the soldiers.

Women's Lives

Women did not play a large public role in colonial American society. They could not vote and they rarely owned property or a business, unless they inherited it from their husbands. Their lives focused on their families and running the household.

Colonial families were much larger than today's. The average mother might have six to eight children. Children were born in the home, and disease and other medical problems killed many women during childbirth. Along with taking care of their children, mothers had to help run the farm, cook, and sew. Daughters were expected to help with the daily chores, and few went to school outside the home. Female slaves worked with men in the field or as servants in the home.

Life was somewhat easier for wealthier women, since they could hire servants or buy slaves to help take care of their children and their homes. Working as a servant was one of the few occupations available to young women, although some did earn a living by doing such jobs as sewing and weaving. Rich young girls might receive a better education, but they were expected to marry and start their own family, not look for a job.

During the American Revolution, many women supported the Patriot cause. Some wealthy women raised money to help feed and clothe the soldiers. In the field, soldiers' wives and other women traveled with the military, doing chores and nursing the sick. Some of these camp followers also joined their husbands in battle.

After the war, women did not win any new rights, though more did attend school. The Declaration of Independence said all men were created equal; it took more than a century for women to begin to win their political and social equality in the United States.

● *See also John Adams, Family Life, Eliza Pinckney, Betsy Ross, School Life*

Colonial women spent most of their time caring for their families. This woman is peeling apples, perhaps preparing to bake a pie.

Yorktown

Six years of fighting between British and Americans forces led to the last major battle of the American Revolution, at Yorktown, Virginia. On October 19, 1781, surrounded by American and French troops on land and French warships off the coast, British forces surrendered to George Washington.

The American victory came after a long campaign that began months before. In August, Washington and French troops led by Comte Jean Baptiste de Rochambeau began marching to Virginia to meet up with a French fleet. Another French army, led by the Marquis de Lafayette, was already fighting British troops in the state.

Before the Yorktown campaign, the British had fought well in the Carolinas. Their commander, Lord Charles Cornwallis, then moved north into Virginia and continued to attack. This move started an argument between Cornwallis and his commander, Sir Henry Clinton, who wanted Cornwallis to stay in North Carolina. Clinton finally allowed Cornwallis to set up a base in Yorktown, overlooking a river that emptied into Chesapeake Bay. Lafayette and his troops followed Cornwallis as he moved toward Yorktown.

By the end of September, Washington and his French allies joined together outside Yorktown with more than 16,000 troops. The French fleet was already in the bay, having driven off the British navy and landed 3,000 troops. Washington's forces dug trenches around the British, then began firing huge French cannons. Over several weeks, Washington led his troops closer to the British camp. Finally, before the Americans could launch a last devastating attack, Cornwallis surrendered. About 8,000 British troops were taken prisoner.

After the surrender, a U.S. colonel wrote that the Americans "could scarcely walk for jumping

and dancing and singing" as they celebrated their success. British and American troops fought several scattered battles afterward, but the victory at Yorktown broke Great Britain's will to continue the war.

The Americans had won their independence.

• *See also British Army, Foreign Aid, Virginia, George Washington*

> *With French ships behind them (on the right) American troops in front of them (on the left), British forces at Yorktown had nowhere to run.*

ARRANGING A SURRENDER

George Washington and Lord Cornwallis (*red coat, above*) exchanged several letters before agreeing on the details of the British surrender. As Cornwallis tried to get the best arrangements he could, Washington seemed to grow impatient. He wrote Cornwallis that he would not allow some British and German troops to return to Europe as Cornwallis requested, and that all ships and their supplies would be turned over to the French and Americans. Washington ended by saying. "Your Lordship will be pleased to signify your determination either to accept or reject the proposals now offered, in the course of two hours from the deliver of this letter...or a renewal of hostilities may take place."

•••

Glossary

allies–friends or supporters, especially during a war

apprentices–workers who learn a skill from a more experienced person

arsenal–place where weapons are stored

artillery–cannons and other large guns used on a battlefield

bayonets–long blade attached to the end of a gun barrel

cabinet–group of advisors to a leader

campaign–series of battles fought in one region

casualties–soldiers killed or wounded during a battle

confederation–union of equal groups or states

delegates–people chosen to represent others at a meeting or convention

diplomat–government representative in a foreign country

duel–a one-on-one battle, often fought with pistols or swords

epidemic–a sudden, fast spread of a dangerous disease over a wide population

expeditions–long trip taken for trade or exploration

Federalist–supporter of a strong national government

feminist–a person who works to ensure equal rights for women

flax–the material of a certain plant that was used to make cloth or clothing

frontiersman–peson who explores a part of a region with few settlers

inoculating–giving medical treatment, involving a shot, to prevent certain diseases

legislative–relating to the passing of laws

levied–collected a fine or tax

libel–purposely publishing or saying facts or words you know are not true

mercantilism–British policy that required colonies to send natural resource to Great Britain and buy finished products in return

midwives–trained experts who assist during a birth

militia–part-time military force composed of local citizens

missionaries–members of a religious group sent out to recruit new members

negotiated–discussed differences to reach an agreement

pacifists–people who does not believe in war or violence

Patriots–people who supported American political freedom before and during the American Revolution

privateers–privately owned ships given government permission to attack enemy ships during wartime

radicals–people with extreme beliefs not held by most members of a community

ratify–approve by a vote

repealed–overturned a law

sachem–leader of a North American tribe

salutary neglect–British policy of the 18th century that allowed American colonies to ignore some laws without being punished

treaty–a document signed by two nations, agreeing to certain terms; often used to end a war or dispute.

wigwams–a style of Native American housing resembling an igloo

Books for Further Reading

Bigelow, Barbara, and Linda Schmittroth. *American Revolution: Alamanac*. Farmington Hills, MI: UXL, 2000.

Bjornlund, Lydia D. *The Constitution and the Founding of America*. San Diego: Lucent Books, 2000.

Bober, Natalie. *Countdown to Independence: A Revolution of Ideas in England and Her Colonies, 1760-1776*. New York: Atheneum Books for Young Readers, 2001.

Butler, Jon. *Religion in Colonial America*. New York: Oxford University Press, 2000.

Collier, Christopher. *The French and Indian War*. New York: Benchmark Books, 1998.

Dorson, Richard M., ed. *Patriots of the American Revolution: True Accounts by Great Americans, from Ethan Allen to George Rogers Clark*. New York: Gramercy Books, 1998.

Faragher, John Mack, ed. *The Encyclopedia of Colonial and Revolutionary America*. New York: De Capo Press, 1996.

Josephy, Alvin M. Jr. *500 Nations: An Illustrated History of North American Indians*. New York: Alfred A. Knopf, 1994.

Marrin, Albert. *George Washington & the Founding of a Nation*. New York: Dutton Children's Books, 2001.

The Revolutionary War. Ten volumes. Danbury, CT: Grolier Educational, 2001.

Web Sites

The American Revolution

http://www.historyplace.com/unitedstates/revolution//

The History Place provides a timeline of colonial and Revolutionary America, with links to illustrations of some key historical figures.

Archiving Early America

http://www.earlyamerica.com/

A source for documents and illustrations from the 18th century

Colonial America, 1600–1775

http://falcon.jmu.edu/~ramseyil/colonial.htm

This site has links to other Web sites covering specific topics of the era, from military history to information on the 13 American colonies

Colonial Williamsburg

http://www.history.org/index.html

Williamsburg, Virginia, a "living museum" from the colonial era, provides historical information at its Web site.

Liberty! The American Revolution

http://www.pbs.org/ktca/liberty/

A Web site based on the 1997 PBS series about the American Revolution

Library of Congress–The Constitution

http://lcweb2.loc.gov/const/abtconst.html

The site has information on the Constitution and links to other important documents of the era.

Index

Index

Index

Index